BERTOLT BRECHT

Life of Galileo

Translated from the German by
JOHN WILLETT

With Commentary and Notes by
HUGH RORRISON

METHUEN DRAMA

Methuen Student Edition

15 14 13 12 11

This Methuen Student Edition first published in 1986 by Methuen
London Ltd by arrangement with Suhrkamp Verlag, Frankfurt am
Main.
Reissued with a new cover design 1994

Methuen Publishing Limited
215 Vauxhall Bridge Road, London SW1V 1EJ
Reissued with a new cover design 1994

This translation of *Life of Galileo* first published in 1980 by Eyre
Methuen. It has been slightly revised for this edition.
Translation copyright © 1980 by Stefan S. Brecht.
Original work entitled *Leben des Galilei*. Copyright 1940 by Arvid
Englind Teaterforlag, a.b., renewed June 1967 by Stefan S. Brecht.
Copyright © 1955 by Suhrkamp Verlag, Frankfurt am Main.
Commentary and Notes in this edition copyright © 1986 by
Methuen London Ltd.

Front cover photograph shows Ernst Busch as Galileo
(Photo: Percy Paukschta)

Papers used by Methuen Publishing Limited
are natural, recyclable products made from wood grown in
sustainable forests. The manufacturing processes conform to
the environmental regulations of the country of origin

Printed and bound in Great Britain by
Cox & Wyman Ltd, Reading, Berkshire

Brecht, Bertolt
  Life of Galileo.
  I. Title   II. Willet, John   III. Leben des
    Galilei. *English*
    832'.912   PT2603.R39

ISBN 0-413-57780-5

*Thanks are due to John Willet, and to Herta Ramthun of the
Brecht Archive, for help in the preparation of this edition.*

Contents

Photos of Brecht's own productions with
Charles Laughton and Ernst Busch
appear on pages iv, xliv and 129—132.
They are reproduced by courtesy of the
Bertolt Brecht-Archiv, Berlin.

Scene 8. Galileo (Charles Laughton) and the Little Monk. *Photos: Ruth Berlau*

Bertolt Brecht 1898–1956

Brecht's life falls into three distinct phases demarcated by his forced exile from his native Germany during the Hitler years. From 1898-1933 he is in Germany; from 1933-1947 he is in exile in various parts of the world; in 1947 he returns to Europe, first to Switzerland then to Berlin.

Germany

1898   Eugen Berthold Friedrich Brecht born on 10 February at Augsburg where his father was an employee and later director of the Haindl paper mill.

1908   Brecht goes to Augsburg Grammar School (Realgymnasium) where he is an indifferent pupil and a rebel in his quiet way, numbering among his friends Caspar Neher, later his designer. Brecht was almost expelled for taking a dismissive, anti-patriotic line when set an essay with the title 'It is a sweet and honourable thing to die for one's country'.

1917   Brecht enrols as a medical student at Munich University, where he also attends Arthur Kutscher's theatre seminar. He samples the bohemian literary life of the city.

1918   Brecht is conscripted and serves as a medical orderly, though he still lives at home. He writes *Baal*, a rumbustious, even outrageous dramatic tribute to natural drives and anarchic sexuality, and does theatre reviews for the local newspaper, *Augsburger Neueste Nachrichten.*

1919   Brecht writes *Drums in the Night.* He meets the comedian Karl Valentin, the theatre director Erich Engel, and actresses Elisabeth Bergner, Blandine Ebinger, Carola Neher and Marianne Zoff.

1920   Brecht visits Berlin.

1921   Brecht's registration at Munich University is cancelled. An attempt to make himself known in literary circles in Berlin ends with him in hospital suffering from malnutrition. His new friendship with Arnolt Bronnen, the playwright, leads him to change the spelling of his name to Bertolt, or Bert.

1922   Brecht marries Marianne Zoff. He writes *In the Jungle of Cities*.

1923   Brecht's daugher Hanne is born. The activities of Hitler's National Socialists are hotly discussed in Brecht's Munich circle. The first productions of *In the Jungle of Cities* and *Baal* take place in Munich and Leipzig respectively.

1924   Brecht directs Christopher Marlow's *Edward II* which he and Lion Feuchtwanger had adapted. He was already using certain devices (plot summaries before scenes, white face make-up to indicate fear) to induce criticial detachment in actors and audience. He finally settles in Berlin and is taken on as dramaturg (literary adviser) at Max Reinhardt's Deutsches Theater. The actress Helene Weigel bears him a son, Stefan.

1925   Klabund's *The Chalk Circle*, premiered at Frankfurt and Hanover in January, is directed in Berlin in October by Max Reinhardt with Elisabeth Bergner in the female lead.

1926   *Man equals Man* premiered at Darmstadt and Dusseldorf. Brecht's work on a play (which he never finished) called *Joe Fleischhacker*, which was to deal with the Chicago Wheat Exchange, leads him to the study of Marx as the only adequate method of analysing the workings of capitalism.

1927   Brecht divorces Marianne Zoff. He works with Erwin Piscator, the pioneer of communist political theatre in Germany, on a dramatisation of Hasek's novel *The Good Soldier Schweik*.

1928   *The Threepenny Opera*, music by Kurt Weill, words by Brecht (based on a translation of John Gay's *Beggar's Opera* by Brecht's friend and collaborator Elisabeth Hauptmann) opens at the Theater am Schiffbauerdamm and becomes the hit of the season. Brecht had provocatively transferred bourgeois manners to a Soho criminal setting.

1929   Brecht marries Helene Weigel. *The Baden-Baden Cantata* is staged at the Baden-Baden Music Festival, music by Hindemith.

1930   Brecht's daughter Barbara born. His Lehrstück or didactic play, *The Measures Taken*, is given its first performance in Berlin. The communist didactic plays for amateur performance were intended to clarify the ideas of the performers as much as the audience. The first performance of *The Rise and Fall of the City of Mahagonny*, and opera with words by Brecht and music by Kurt Weill causes a riot as the Nazis voice their criticism at Leipzig. In his notes on the opera Brecht tabulates the differences between the traditional *dramatic* (or Aristotelian) and the new *epic* (or non-Aristotelian) theatre at which he is aiming,

1931   Brecht completes *St Joan of the Stockyards* (first performed in 1959).

1932   Brecht's only film, *Kuhle Wampe*, is held up by the censor. His dramatisation of Maxim Gorky's novel *The Mother* is performed by a left-wing collective in Berlin, music by Hanns Eisler. It demonstrates the development of a worker's mother towards proletarian class-consciousness. Beginning of Brecht's friendship with Margarete Steffin. Brecht studies Marxism under the dissident communist Karl Korsch.

Exile

1933   The Nazis come to power. The night after the German parliament building (the Reichstag) is burnt down, Brecht flees with his family to Prague. He moves to Vienna, then Zurich, finally settling on the island of Fyn in Denmark. His friendship with Ruth Berlau begins.

1934   Brecht visits London. The themes of flight and exile enter his poetry.

1935   Brecht is stripped of his German citizenship. He visits Moscow where he talks to the Soviet dramatist Sergei Tretiakov about the 'alienation effect'. He attends the International Writers' Conference in Paris. He visits New York to look in on a production of *The Mother*, which does not meet with his approval.

1936   Brecht attends the International Writers' Conference in London. He writes anti-fascist poetry.

1937   Brecht attends the International Writers' Conference in Paris.

1938   Franco's right-wing Falangists emerge as the likely victors in the Spanish Civil War and Chamberlain signs away the Sudetenland in the Munich Treaty in an effort to appease Hitler. *Fear and Misery of the Third Reich* is given its first performance in Paris. Brecht writes *The Earth Moves* in three weeks ending on 23 November. He revises it with the assistance of Margarete Steffin, adds a fourteenth scene and retitles it *Life of Galileo*.

1939   In a radio interview with scientists of the Niels Bohr

Institute Brecht hears of the discovery of a great new source of energy, nuclear fission. His first response is positive. In April he moves to Stockholm with his family. He finishes writing *Mother Courage and Her Children*.

1940   German forces march into Denmark. In Lidingo Brecht completes *The Augsburg Chalk Circle*, a short story set in the Thirty Years War. Brecht's household moves to Helsinki in Finland where his friendship with the writer Hella Wuolijoki begins.

1941   Brecht completes *Mr Puntila and his Man Matti*, *The Good Person of Szechwan* and *The Resistable Rise of Arturo Ui*. He writes war poetry and 'Finnish Epigrams'. Leaving Finland Brecht travels through the Soviet Union via Leningrad and Moscow (where Margarete Steffin dies) to Vladivostock and sails to the U.S.A. He arrives in Los Angeles in July and settles with his family in Santa Monica. He makes contact with other exiles (Heinrich Mann, Lion Feuchtwanger and Fritz Lang, the film director) and with the natives (Orson Welles). First performance of *Mother Courage and her Children* in neutral Switzerland.

1942   Brecht prepares his *Poems in Exile* for publication. He participates in the anti-war, anti-fascist activities of exile groups. He meets Charles Laughton.

1943   The first performance of *The Good Person of Szechwan* and of *Life of Galileo* take place in Zurich.

1944   Brecht becomes a member of the newly formed Council for a Democratic Germany. In April Jed Harris, an American producer and director, enquires about *Galileo*, and Brecht looks afresh at its 'moral'. He writes the first version of *The Caucasian Chalk Circle*, and almost immediately starts reworking it. He studies Arthur Waley's translations of Chinese poetry. In September he begins to revise *Galileo* with Charles Laughton.

1945   *Fear and Misery of the Third Reich* is performed in New York under the title *The Private Life of the Master Race*. Brecht and Laughton complete the English version of *Galileo* but the dropping of the atomic bombs on Hiroshima and Nagasaki in August gives rise to another revision which stresses the social responsibility of the scientist.

1946   The first performance of Brecht's adaptation of Webster's *The Duchess of Malfi* takes place in Boston.

1947   Charles Laughton appears in the title role of *Life of Galileo* in Beverly Hills and New York. Brecht appears before the *House Committee on Unamerican Activities* and proves himself a master of ambiguity when cross-examined about his communist sympathies.

Return

Brecht and Helene Weigel go to Zurich, leaving their son Stefan, who is an American citizen, in the U.S.A. Brecht meets Max Frisch, his old friend and designer Caspar Neher, and the playwright Carl Zuckmayer.

1948   Brecht's adaptation of *Antigone of Sophocles* is performed in Chur, Switzerland, and *Mr Puntila and his Man Matti* is given its first performance in Zurich. He publishes the *Little Organum for the Theatre*. Brecht travels to Berlin and starts rehearsals of *Mother Courage* at the Deutsches Theater in the Soviet sector of the city. *The Caucasian Chalk Circle* is first performed in Eric and Maja Bentley's English translation by students at 'Jorthfield, Minnesota.

1949   *Mother Courage* opens at the Deutsches Theater with Helene Weigel in the title role. Brecht visits Zurich again before settling in Berlin. The *Berliner Ensemble*, Brecht and Helene Weigel's own state-subsidised company, is formed and opens with *Puntila*. At Gottfried von Einem's suggestion Brecht applies for an Austrian passport (H. Weigel is Austrian) as Caspar Neher had already done.

1951   *The Mother* is performed by the *Berliner Ensemble*. Brecht finishes the first version of his adaptation of Shakespeare's *Coriolanus*.

1953   Ethel and Julius Rosenberg are executed in the U.S.A. for betraying atomic secrets to the Russians. Brecht is elected President of this German section of the PEN Club, the international writers' association. On 17 June there are strikes and demonstrations protesting about working conditions in the German Democratic Republic. Brecht writes a letter to the Secretary of the Socialist Unity Party which is released to the press in a doctored form.

1954   The trial of atomic physicist Robert J. Oppenheimer begins in the U.S.A., and Albert Einstein writes an article inveighing against this modern 'inquisition', but the idea that science is subordinate to state security gains currency. Brecht is awarded the Stalin Peace Prize. The Berliner Ensemble moves into its own home, the Theater am Schiffbauerdamm (where he had triumphed with *The Threepenny Opera* in 1928), and performs *The Caucasian Chalk Circle*. The prologue, *The Struggle for the Valley*, is now designated as Act I. Brecht makes public his objections to the Paris Treaty (which incorporated the Federal Republic of Germany into Nato) and to re-armament in general. The Berliner Ensemble's productions of *Mother Courage* and Kleist's *The Broken Pitcher* are enthusiastically received as the highlights of the Paris Théâtre des Nations festival. *Mother Courage* is awarded the prizes for best play and best production.

1955   In December Brecht begins rehearsals of *Life of Galileo* using the third version of the play, a modified retranslation into German of Laughton's English version. Ernst Busch takes the title role. Harry Buckwitz, directing the West German premiere of *The Caucasian Chalk Circle* at Frankfurt, omits *The Struggle for the Valley* as politically inopportune.

1956   Brecht's health prevents him from carrying on with *Galileo* and he hands over the direction to Erich Engel. Brecht is preparing the Berliner Ensemble, which by that time has become generally recognised as the foremost progressive theatre in Europe, for a visit to London when he dies of a heart attack on 14 August. The visit goes ahead and *Mother Courage*, *The Caucasian Chalk Circle*, and *Trumpets and Drums* are presented at the Palace Theatre at the end of August for a short season — a landmark in Brecht's reception in the United Kingdom.

1957   *Life of Galileo* opens at the Berliner Ensemble on 15 January in sets by Caspar Neher and with music by Eisler.

Plot

Galileo expounds the Copernican system to his housekeeper's son as an element in the new thinking that is about to revolutionize science and society. He passes off the telescope, a Dutch invention, as his own to extract a raise from his Venetian employers. The telescope provides him with proof that the Copernican system is accurate, and he moves to Florence in search of more money and scope for research. The Florentine scholars reject his ideas and the Church forces him to drop his research on the solar system. He resumes it to popular acclaim when a mathematician becomes Pope, but the Inquisition forces him to disown the theory that the earth revolves round the sun. Under virtual house arrest he produces a major scientific treatise and smuggles a clandestine copy to the free world, yet he dismisses his research as a vice on a par with his gluttony. Looking back on his recantation, he is convinced that his failure to give a moral lead to scientists when he had the chance has corrupted modern science at its source.

Scene 1
Padua, 1609. Stripped to the waist for his morning wash, Galileo explains the Ptolemaic system to Andrea Sarti, his housekeeper's son. It represents, he says, an old theory, which placed the earth at the centre of the universe and let the sun and planets revolve round it. Recent thinking suggests that the earth revolves round the sun, carrying all mankind, regardless of status, round with it. He demonstrates with a chair and a washstand how the new Copernican system works. Mrs Sarti announces a new pupil and reminds Galileo that there are bills to be paid. She scolds Galileo for confusing her already scatter-brained son. She goes off and Andrea's shrewd questions force Galileo to demonstrate with an apple how the earth can rotate without our noticing it. Galileo's new pupil, a rich young man called Ludovico Marsili whose mother wants him to have a smattering of science presents himself. He agrees to Galileo's exorbitant fee and casually mentions a funny new contraption with two lenses he saw in Amsterdam. Galileo takes note of how it works. The procurator of the University of Padua tells Galileo his

application for an increase in salary has been turned down. He reminds the disgruntled Galileo that in Venice he is safe from the Inquisition and that the city fathers will always pay for a practical invention. Galileo tells him he has one almost ready, and complains that he has no time to develop ideas he picks up while he is working in the Venice arsenal. When the Procurator has gone, Galileo reminds Andrea not to talk about the new theories outside. Andrea protests that they are true, Galileo tells him that they are only attractive but unproven hypotheses, and that the authorities have forbidden them. He sets up two lenses Andrea has fetched from the lens-grinder and Andrea tells him that he can see the words 'by the grace of God' on the campanile bells. With his tongue in his cheek Galileo remarks that that should be good for 500 scudi.

Scene 2
Galileo presents a telescope to the Doge and other civic dignitaries at the Arsenal as the fruit of prolonged research. As the top Venetians examine the potentially profitable instrument, Galileo tells his friend Sagredo that the telescope looks like providing data which will prove the Copernican theory. It has already shown him that the moon does not generate its own light. He then socializes with the Senators, and Marsili observes ironically that he is beginning to see what science is about.

Scene 3
On Jan. 10, 1610, Galileo shows his friend Sagredo the mountains on the moon and explains to him that it is, like the earth, a star which derives its light from the sun. Sagredo is aghast and reminds Galileo that only ten years earlier Giordano Bruno was burnt by the Inquisition for the same heresy. Galileo is confident that things will be different now that he can show physical proof. He remarks that mankind can note in its diary that today he, Galileo, got rid of heaven. The Procurator comes to report indignantly that a shipload of cheap telescopes has just arrived from Holland. Galileo admits he knew of the Dutch invention, claims to have improved it and justifies his trick by explaining that they pay him less than a carter. Galileo shows Sagredo the moons of Jupiter through the telescope and the two men make the calculations that show that Jupiter has satellites. Sagredo warns him that his discovery is theological dynamite, but Galileo insists jubilantly that humanity will accept rational proof. Mrs Sarti is called but she refuses to bring Andrea to look through the telescope, though she does

confirm Galileo's contention that smaller objects revolve around
greater ones. When Virginia asks to look through the telescope he
tells her it is not a toy. He then reports that he is going to name his
new stars after the Grand Duke of Florence and ask him to employ
him. Sagredo warns him that the city run by monks will be his
doom, and tells him that his credulity in politics is the equal of his
scepticism in science. Galileo stubbornly insists that he is going to
Florence, and the scene ends with a projection of his obsequious
letter to the Grand Duke.

Scene 4
In Florence Mrs Sarti anticipates disaster as she prepares for Galileo
to receive the court. The nine year old Grand Duke Cosimo arrives
ahead of the university party and goes in to look at the telescope
with Andrea. They end up fighting over the astronomical models.
When the court and scholars arrive Galileo explains that the Medicean
Stars he has discovered orbiting Jupiter prove that the Ptolemaic
system is wrong. The Philosopher says the proper procedure
requires a formal debate on the proposition 'can such planets exist',
and the Mathematician cites the ancient theory that stars revolving
round a centre other than the earth, or without a support in the
sky cannot exist. The philosopher is about to launch into a Latin
disquisition on the topic, 'are such planets necessary?' when Galileo
objects that Federzoni, his lens-grinder will not understand.
Eloquently but superciliously, the Philosopher describes the
Aristotelian view of the universe in the vernacular. When Galileo
invites Cosimo to look for himself, the Mathematician queries the
reliability of the telescope, and asks why there should suddenly be
free-floating stars in the unalterable heavens. Andrea stalks out
saying that the visitors are stupid. When Galileo asks them to use
their eyes, the Mathematician replies that he always does — to read
Aristotle. Galileo insists desperately that they must move with the
times and pursue the truth, but the Philosopher demurs: the truth
could lead anywhere. Galileo turns to the Grand Duke and tells him
that hitherto unquestioned truths are tottering everywhere under
the impact of empirical evidence. The practical procedures
employed in the Venice dockyards and the questing spirit of recent
explorers embody the supreme curiosity that was the true glory of
Ancient Greece. However the Grand Duke is shepherded out
before he has a chance to look through the telescope. As he leaves,
the Chamberlain remarks that Galileo's claims will be referred to the
papal astronomer in Rome.

Scene 5

Virginia is sent home from the convent because the city is stricken
with the plague. The Grand Duke sends a carriage and Galileo
packs the children off to the country but insists on staying himself
to finish his work. Mrs Sarti stays with him.

Galileo goes into the street to look for Mrs Sarti and discovers
that she left the house when she felt ill so that he would not be
infected. She is in hospital. He criticises the authorities' practice of
hushing up epidemics until they get out of hand and then isolating
the victims without care. Andrea returns, having walked for three
days to get back, and Galileo sends him to fetch some reference
books he needs.

Scene 6

It is Rome, 1616. In the Collegium Romanum monks, priests and
Catholic scholars joke hilariously at Galileo's expense, pretending
the rotating earth makes them dizzy. Two papal astronomers
emerge from conclave, displeased that the church's greatest astronomer, Christopher Clavius, is taking Galileo's hypotheses seriously.
There is general agreement that the new science degrades the earth
and debases humanity. Galileo, isolated on one side, drops his
proving stone to bolster his faith in reason. The Very Old Cardinal
dodders on. He claims that man is and always has been the crown
of creation which explains why God sent his son to him. He notices
in Galileo a resemblance to Giordano Bruno. At the effort of
proclaiming he is not just any old creature on some insignificant star
he collapses. At this moment Clavius emerges. The Little Monk
tells Galileo that Clavius has accepted his findings and declared that
the theologians must come to terms with them. Galileo claims this
as a victory for reason and not for himself. As he leaves the Cardinal
Inquisitor goes to examine the telescope.

Scene 7

Galileo is a celebrity at a ball at Cardinal Bellarmin's house. His
daughter Virginia, who is now engaged to Ludovico, is delighted at
their new social status. Galileo tells two monks who are playing
chess it is time they adopted the liberated new rules. Even the Very
Old Cardinal now greets Galileo. Cardinals Bellarmin and Barberini,
masked as lamb and dove respectively, engage him in conversation.
Barberini tests Galileo with astronomical allusions from the Bible.
He is impressed with Galileo's answers. Bellarmin states his belief
that only doctrines that conflict with the Scriptures need be
opposed. After a short duel with Biblical quotations Barberini

welcomes Galileo to the fleshpots of Rome. Galileo declines his invitation to look over the available ladies and continues to discuss astronomy with Bellarmin who suggests that God might have devised a random, asymmetrical universe. Galileo counters that he would in that case have equipped man with a random, asymmetrical mind. After telling the scribes that what he is saying is off the record, Bellarmin tells Galileo that revising basic astronomical concepts could jeopardise the peasantry's faith in the Bible and with it the entire fabric of society. Galileo protests that he is a faithful son of the church and suggests that some of the readings of the Bible rather than the Scriptures themselves could be faulty. Bellarmin tells him that the doctrine of Copernicus, on which his theories are based, has been declared heretical, though he may continue his research on the understanding that it is legitimate to explore but impossible to know. When Galileo angrily asserts that nothing harms faith so much as invoking it, Bellarmin warns him not to go too far. As the two cardinals go off the Inquisitor collects a transcript of the conversation from the monks who have been taking notes and chats with Virginia about the presumptuousness of recent atronomical thinking. Finally he ascertains who her father confessor is.

Scene 8
The Little Monk tells Galileo that he is unable to reconcile his observations of the moons of Jupiter with the decree that Galileo's theories are heretical, so, after mature consideration, he is giving up astronomy. In so doing, he is thinking of his parents whose dutiful life of grinding toil would be made absurd at a stroke if the faith were discredited in any way. The Church is protecting them from the new doctrines out of sheer goodness. Galileo expostulates that the reason for the monk's parents' poverty is that they are paying for the Church's wars. Otherwise they could live in plenty and develop the virtues of affluence in a world made fertile by science. The monk is appalled but Galileo insists that the authorities have effectively bribed him not to stir up the lower orders. Much as he admires the divine patience of the common people he deplores their lack of divine wrath. When the monk suggests that the truth might somehow get through on its own. Galileo replies that it needs to be forced through. He shows the monk his new paper on the tides and it engrosses him instantly. Galileo promises to explain any difficult points to him.

Scene 9

Eight years later Virginia and Mrs Sarti are sewing while Andrea sets up the day's experiments on floating bodies. Virginia feels Galileo has seen the error of his ways since he has published nothing for eight years. Filippo Mucius, an ex-pupil calls to explain why he contradicted Copernicus in his recent book. Galileo rejects his explanation and tells him that to know the truth and deny it is the mark of a crook. Mucius goes out crestfallen. Virginia confides to Mrs Sarti that she has consulted an astrologer and knows what her future holds. The Rector of the university brings Galileo a book on sunspots which are in the forefront of scientific interest everywhere but Galileo refuses to comment, saying he has no wish to be roasted over a fire. He turns to his experiment on floating bodies and disproves one of Aristotle's findings. Ludovico Marsili arrives unexpectedly and Galileo pretends not to recognize him. He then calls for a jug of old Sicilian wine as Virginia goes off to put on her wedding dress for Ludovico to see. Ludovico congratulates Galileo for not joining in the sunspot controversy which Clavius feels will reopen the 'earth round the sun' issue, and tells him that the Pope is dying and is likely to be succeeded by Cardinal Barberini. The prospect of a mathematician in the Vatican induces Galileo to resume his work on the solar system. He insults Ludovico, even after Mrs Sarti has told him that Virginia's future happiness is at stake. Ludovico reminds him that as a landowner he cannot tolerate any flouting of church doctrine and leaves. Galileo turns to his telescope to see whether sunspots will support his hypothesis that the sun rotates. Virginia returns in her wedding dress and faints when she sees Ludovico has gone. Galileo pursues his experiment unmoved.

Scene 10

In 1632 a carnival ballad-singer sings the song of 'Ye Horrible Doctrine and Opinions of Messer Galileo Galilei'. It is a comic account of how Galileo turned the biblical version of creation in which small objects revolve round greater ones upside down, so that the earth now revolves round the sun and the master round his servants. He sketches a future in which the artisan will consume the fruits of his own labour. The singer's wife jokes that she has taken advantage of her liberty to try out another man, then the two in unison incite their audience to do as they please. The ballad-singer demonstrates the earth's orbit with a model sun and a pumpkin, then carnival floats with figures ridiculing the Grand

Duke of Florence and glorifying Galileo 'the bible-buster' are
wheeled on and greeted with great hilarity.

Scene 11
In 1633 Galileo and his daughter are waiting to hand over the
'Dialogues of the Two World Systems' to the Grand Duke. Virginia
points out a man who is shadowing them. The rector of the
university avoids them. Vanni, an ironfounder for whom Galileo
has designed a furnace tells Galileo that the authorities hold him
responsible for the recent spate of anti-Bible pamphlets. Galileo
protests that the Bible is his favourite reading. Vanni assures him
that he has the support of the northern manufacturers who want to
keep abreast of technical and commercial advances abroad. Galileo
refuses to see any danger and insultingly dismisses Vanni's offer to
help him escape. The Florentine official on the door pointedly
ignores Galileo. When the Inquisitor and the Grand Duke emerge
the latter declines to accept Galileo's book. All this terrifies Virginia
and Galileo tells her to control herself. He has a cart waiting next
door to smuggle him out of the city. As he turns to go a high
official tells him that an Inquisition coach is waiting to take him
to Rome.

Scene 12
The Pope gives an audience to the Cardinal Inquisitor in his
robing room at the Vatican. In his undergarments he rejects the
Inquisitor's suggestions that he should interfere with the new
science. The Inquisitor reminds him that mathematics is not the
problem, but the spirit of insubordination and doubt that science
has propagated. The church faces a crisis. Germany has been ravaged
by religious wars for fifteen years and the movement generated by
Galileo threatens to make God unnecessary. The Pope agrees that it
is in poor taste for Galileo to write in Italian. The Inquisitor
observes that they will have to let the north Italian ports use
Galileo's star charts. When the Pope protests that they cannot
accept the charts and condemn the theories on which they are
based, the Inquisitor replies that material interests are involved and
there is no other way. The shuffling of the faithful who are waiting
for the Pope can be heard. The Pope is reluctant to move against the
greatest physicist of the day. The Inquisitor replies that he is a man
of the flesh who will recant at the mere sight of the instruments of
torture and reminds the Pope that though Galileo fulfilled the
church's conditions with his last book he nonetheless put Aristotle's
(and the Church's) case in the mouth of a fool. The Pope agrees

that this was impertinent. In full regalia he identifies with the Inquisitor's position and agrees that Galileo shall be shown the instruments and his doctrine declared heretical.

Scene 13

On 22 June 1633 Galileo's pupils await the outcome of his examination by the Inquisition. Galileo has been twenty-four days in prison. Andrea is convinced that he will never recant. Federzoni reckons they have the power to force him. The Little Monk reflects that Galileo should have stayed in Venice and reminisces about Galileo's love of beauty, in particular the poetry of Horace. Andrea mimics Galileo's plea to the Collegium Romanum for 'a little reason'. The Inquisition agent announces that he is expected to recant around five o'clock, when the great bell of St Mark's will be tolled. Andrea responds by declaiming Galileo's doctrine loudly. At three minutes past they begin to rejoice that he has held firm, and stupidity has been defeated. Then the bell rings out and the town crier's voice is heard proclaiming Galileo's recantation of his view that the sun is the centre of the cosmos. Galileo appears, almost unrecognizable after his ordeal. Andrea shouts that it is an unhappy land that has no heroes, then sits down feeling ill. Galileo calls for a glass of water for him, and, as Andrea is escorted out, rephrases his complaint — it is an unhappy land that has need of heroes. The scene ends with a reading of Galileo's paper on the relative durability of large and small machines.

Scene 14

Galileo has been living in seclusion for some years at his country house near Florence. A goose is unexpectedly delivered and while its liver is being cooked with thyme and apples Galileo, as his devotional exercise of the day, dictates comments for the archbishop on items of church policy and selected biblical quotations. Virginia takes them down, oblivious to their irony. Andrea Sarti arrives unexpectedly. He has been estranged since the recantation and is on his way to Holland to work with Fabricius, at whose request he has called to enquire about Galileo's health. He reports that Descartes abandoned his treatise on light when Galileo recanted, and that Federzoni is back grinding lenses and the Little Monk back in the bosom of the Church. Galileo laughs cynically, then sends Virginia to see to the goose and reveals that he has completed the 'Discorsi'. The manuscript has been confiscated, but he has made a secret transcript which he gives to Andrea, telling him to claim it was leaked from the Holy Office. Andrea revises his opinion of Galileo, assuming that his recantation was a deliberate ploy to escape from the shackles of the church and quietly get on with the business of science. Galileo corrects him — he recanted purely because he was afraid of torture. Andrea condones this too, since it enabled him to go on contributing to science. Galileo dismisses this in an outburst of self-condemnation. Science, he says, is involved on two fronts. It seeks to understand the physical universe but also to better the lot of mankind and change society. The ruling classes seek to control the scientists and make them serve their interests. Galileo bowed to this control and threw away a unique chance to establish a 'Hippocratic' code of conduct for scientists and thus to secure the benefits of science for all of mankind. Galileo has betrayed his profession and spawned a breed of inventive dwarfs who will sell their discoveries to the highest bidder to use or misuse as they please. Virginia returns, Andrea takes his leave with the 'Discorsi' under his coat and Galileo tucks into the goose.

Scene 15
At the Italian frontier customs officials check Andrea's luggage. A child warns him that he is sitting outside a witch's house. A second child who is too poor to go to school contradicts this and a third says she flies through the air at night. Andrea is openly reading Galileo's manuscript. He claims it is a work of Aristotle, and a guard takes a perfunctory look at it and lets Andrea pass because he has taxes to collect. As he leaves Italy Andrea instructs the boys to use their eyes and assures them that people cannot fly, or at least the machine that would enable them to do so has not been invented yet.

Commentary

Moral

In his diary on 6 April 1944 Brecht noted that on looking at *Life of Galileo* again after an enquiry about it from Jed Harris, an American producer, he had misgivings:

> . . . precisely because i was trying to follow history here and had no personal moral interest, a moral emerged, and i am not too happy about it.

This refers to the first version of *Life of Galileo* which Brecht had written in three weeks in November 1938 under the title *The Earth Moves*. It was retitled in the course of a minor revision early in 1939. Brecht was living in Denmark in exile at that time, and events had made it clear that the Nazi regime in Germany was not going to disappear as quickly as some of the more sanguine left-wing predictions had suggested. Britain and France had just sought to appease Hitler by signing away part of Czechoslovakia to the Germans at Munich in September, so strengthening the Nazis' hand that any semblance of open opposition in Germany became impossible.

Brecht asked himself in 1939 whether writing *Life of Galileo* was a piece of escapism on his part, surrounded as he was by increasing barbarism and the seemingly inevitable prospect of war. On reflection he thought not. Galileo too lived in a period of historical crisis. At the beginning of the play he blithely assumes that he is standing on the threshold of a new age. Since his conversion to marxism in 1926 Brecht had been hoping for a new age of another kind, the establishment of a socialist state in Germany like the one the 1917 October Revolution had brought into existence in Russia. In seventeenth century Italy the Inquisition supervened, in twentieth century Germany, Hitler. This provided the basic historical parallel. Galileo in the first version of the play was presented as a scientist who falls foul of an authoritarian regime and, under threat of torture, declares his scientific findings to be invalid. This estranges his assistants and perplexes the scientific world, but it is revealed at the end of the play to be a strategy for survival.

As the scene which corresponds to scene 14 of the present text opens, Galileo's attempt to smuggle his secret copy of the *Discorsi* out of Italy with the aid of a stove-fitter has just been thwarted by the authorities, when Andrea's arrival unexpectedly provides him with the messenger he needs. It turns out that since his recantation Galileo has not only carried on his researches but also outwitted his supervisors. Brecht's musical collaborator Hanns Eisler saw in this Galileo the incarnation of 'low cunning for survival', so his behaviour could be construed as a model for the intellectuals trapped in the Third Reich who could work underground while they waited for the overthrow of the regime.

In a sense there is of course something of Brecht's own plight too in Galileo's situation. His emigration put him out of circulation so that he could only continue his opposition indirectly from abroad. He and Galileo had the common problem of deciding how to respond to political oppression, though Galileo was much nearer the centre of the storm.

This first Galileo was a positive anti-hero who refused to sacrifice himself and lived to fight another day. His actions could be construed as a form of 'inner emigration', a term that was later to be applied to the behaviour of certain non-Nazi artists who stayed in Germany after 1933, but it was not so much this as the implication that scientific research took precedence over social responsibility that Brecht objected to as the inadvertant moral that had crept into the first version of *Life of Galileo*.

At this stage Galileo has a certain kinship with Keuner, another of Brecht's figures whose 'backbone was not for breaking'. *Measures Against Violence*, one of the *Tales of Keuner* was in fact incorporated in the first version. It tells how those in power in a time of lawlessness billet an agent on a certain Herr Egge, and that agent asks Herr Egge if he will serve him. After seven years the agent dies of self-indulgence and Herr Egge drags the corpse outside, redecorates the house, breathes a sigh of relief and only then pronounces his answer: 'No'. The clear implication is that passive resistance is the appropriate and effective response.

It was in this version that the play was given its first performance in Zurich in 1943.

It was only on 27 February, 1939, too late to influence the first version, though he sometimes claimed the contrary, that Brecht heard physicists from the Niels Bohr Institute in Copenhagen on radio discussing the splitting of the atom, but the role of science in World War II, and finally the development of atomic fission for

military uses were to change the moral of *Life of Galileo* when
Brecht returned to it in August 1945 to produce an English
translation with Charles Laughton. Brecht's changing view of
science emerges in his 'Drafts for a Foreword to *Life of Galileo*'.
He had long thought of himself as a kind of scientist and of his
plays as experiments in human behaviour, and he initially shared
the vision he attributes to Galileo of a world in which science can
lighten man's burden. The war changed his perspective. He noted
that wars, among other things, promote the sciences. In Nazi
Germany medical research made use of human guinea-pigs, and
science in general sold out to the regime in return for unlimited
research facilities.

Brecht and Laughton collaborated on the translation and
revision of *Life of Galileo* for over two years. Brecht later called
this a time of unmitigated joy. He saw in Laughton the great actor
who would carry his play to triumph on the New York stage, and
Laughton saw Brecht's play as the vehicle which would end a
bad patch in his acting career. Laughton cut and streamlined the
text, but he also suggested substantial changes, clarifying the
social implications of the argument between Ludovico and Galileo
in scene 9 for example, and putting Galileo's long speech of self-
accusation in scene 14 after the handing over of the *Discorsi* in
such a way as to undercut any positive effect that might have.
Brecht rewrote Galileo's lines in the latter scene to introduce a
new self abasement.

Even the first version, as the critics' response to the Zurich
production showed, did not make it clear to the audience whether
Galileo recanted as a ploy to save his life's work and smuggle it to
freedom, or just out of cowardice. In the American version
Galileo's motivation was altered and clarified. As soon as Andrea
has the *Discorsi* in his hands he concludes that Galileo has foxed
his friends as well as his foes and is morally a step ahead of them
all, the Macchiavellian scientist whose only interest is science.
Galileo cynically disabuses him. He tells him he recanted out of
fear at the sight of the instruments of torture, and in doing so
passed up a unique opportunity to resist authority and assert the
right of science to publish the truth. The consequence of this was
that instead of establishing the principle that the scientist had a
duty to use science in the service of mankind, he introduced the
practice of making science subservient to the ruling classes. In
Brecht's eyes his recantation is a crime, the 'original sin' of the
modern natural sciences which led in a direct line to the abuse of

science by the Nazis, and much further, as we shall see later.

In this second version the moral for the scientist was no longer 'practice low cunning and survive', but 'stand up and be counted in the struggle for a responsible and equitable society'.

Brecht and Laughton had completed their second version of *Life of Galileo* along these lines when the first atomic bomb was dropped on Hiroshima on 6 August 1945. Soon afterwards Brecht wrote:

> The 'atomic' age made its debut at Hiroshima in the middle of our work. Overnight the biography of the founder of the new system of physics read differently.

In fact the debunking of Galileo in the play had already taken place and this appalling new stage in the history of warfare only led to alterations of detail to sharpen the critique.

The Brecht/Laughton text, which was the fruit of a genial collaboration in which Brecht explained the German to the expatriate British actor and he formulated the English text, formed the basis of the final version of *Life of Galileo* when it was translated back into German under the direction of Elisabeth Hauptmann for the 1956 Berliner Ensemble production.

In the climate of the Cold War, with Europe, and in particular West Germany, rearming, Brecht's affirmation that the scientist had a moral responsibility for the use to which his work was put, had a renewed relevance. In 1952 the U.S.A. successfully tested the first hydrogen bomb, and in 1953 J. Robert Oppenheimer, a leading figure in the Los Alamos project which made Hiroshima possible, was declared a security risk because of his scruples about developing further nuclear weapons. The U.S.S.R. acquired the A-bomb in 1946 and went on to develop the H-bomb, and the possibility of a suicidal clash between the super-powers became a real threat. Brecht had every reason to feel his plea for social responsibility in the application of science was still topical as he worked on the third version for a production at the Berliner Ensemble in 1956.

History

Brecht wrote *Life of Galileo* in three weeks in 1939, but it is clear from the historical detail that he had at some time researched the background, and several sources are known, among them the writings of Galileo and Francis Bacon, Emil Wohlwill's *Galileo and his Struggle for the Copernican Doctrine*, A.S. Eddington's

The Nature of the Physical World, and Sir James Jeans' *The Mysterious Universe*. What attracted Brecht to the subject was the clash of ideologies which it represented, with Galileo as the champion of a new spirit of empiricism and untrammelled scientific enquiry and the Church as the defender of the faith. The Church subscribed to the scholastic or Aristotelian view of the world and to the Ptolemaic system, both of which served to reconcile the biblical and the visible universe.

The Ptolemaic system which placed the earth at the centre of the universe had, not unnaturally, been setting insoluble problems for Renaissance astronomers who tried to apply mathematical principles to the movements of the stars, and in 1543 Nicolaus Copernicus, working in Germany, formulated the theory that the earth and planets revolve round the sun. It was only when Giordano Bruno took up this theory and associated it with a kind of pantheism which saw God as a universal and unifying substance rather than a person, that the Church realised that the new theory demolished the notion of a finite universe and threatened the Scriptures. Bruno was excommunicated and burned at the stake in 1600. Galileo subscribes to his pantheism when he says God is 'Within ourselves or nowhere' (p.28) but otherwise Brecht largely ignores the theological controversies which raged at the time. He is interested in Galileo only as the man who laid the groundwork for 'the great age which brought the world the rise of the natural sciences', though by the end of World War II Brecht had come to think that that great epoch was ending. There are two aspects to Galileo's contribution to it. First the experimental method which, as he expounds it to Andrea before they start to study sunspots in scene 9, was to let the facts eliminate all hypotheses but the correct one. This empirical approach developed into rationalism which dominated philosophy in the eighteenth century and in the nine- teenth produced the materialism of Ludwig Feuerbach and the dialectical materialism of Karl Marx. Brecht in a sense makes Galileo embody his own tradition when, in scene 3, he gives him an eighteenth century line worthy of Denis Diderot, 'I believe in human reason'. He also invests him with a flash of his own sardonic wit when he makes him say, 'Today mankind can write in its diary: Got rid of Heaven', though to be fair, his Galileo never challenges the validity of the Bible and contents himself with remarking that contemporary interpretations of it might be faulty. Barberini, also in scene 3, is anachronistically quoting the arch- rationalist Voltaire himself when he says, 'If God did not exist, we should have to invent him'. This empirical, rationalist and materialist strand of thinking was closely bound up with progressive social theories, and influenced both the French and Russian Revolutions. The application of science after Galileo fulfilled what Vanni in scene 11 expects of it and led to the Industrial Revolution and on to modern industrial society of which, apart from its class structure, Brecht in the twenties and thirties broadly approved. He saw Galileo as 'responsible for its technical creation'.

It is within this constellation and not within the framework of religious or theological controversy that Brecht identifies the role of the church. He comments in his notes,

> The church, however, is mainly treated here as a secular establishment. Its specific ideology is being looked at in the light of its function as a prop to practical rule.

The Church functions simply as authority. It has a vested interest in the status quo, indeed its interests are identical with those of the landowners, because any questioning of the religious framework which kept the peasants, if not contented, as least docile in their drudgery, would affect the privileges of the Church just as much as those of the landowners. In the play Ludovico puts the case for the latter, Bellarmin and the Very Old Cardinal for the former. Brecht presents the Church as a power structure, the ideological arm of the ruling class, and the ultimate arbiter in spiritual, intellectual and even political matters.

Galileo

Life of Galileo is the only Brecht play which is based directly on an historical figure. Of the other plays that might be called historical, *Eduard II* is an adaptation of Marlowe, *The Resistible Rise of Arturo Ui* offers a satirical view of Hitler's rise to power in terms of Chicago gangsterdom, *Days of the Commune* recreates an historical event, and the *Lucullus* radio play and opera are very free treatments of ancient history. In *Mother Courage and her Children*, the other historical play he set in the same period as *Life of Galileo*, his fictitious heroine moves among the lower ranks; the famous names of the day, King Gustavus Adolphus of Sweden and Marshall Tilly are mentioned only when they die, and the illustrious Wallenstein is not mentioned at all. *Life of Galileo* takes a turning point in history and shows how it was handled at the top level. According to Sergei Tretiakov the figure of Galileo began to interest Brecht around 1933 when he toyed with the idea of preparing a series of great trials from history for the stage.

The plot follows Galileo's conflict with the Papacy closely, although there is some restructuring, but his character, from the first conception to the final figure is Brecht's own creation and stands in a line of anti-heroes which starts with Baal, and runs through Kragler in *Drums in the Night* and the Cook in *Mother Courage* to Azdak in *The Caucasian Chalk Circle*. These characters all show a brand of hedonism and a rude vigour which Galileo shares. Galileo is established as a physical presence in the first scene when, stripped to the waist, he is rubbed down by Andrea as he makes his optimistic speech about the dawn of a new age. Brecht was determined from the outset to avoid the stereotype of the unworldly professor and establish Galileo as a man with healthy appetites. He likes to eat, his best ideas come to him over a good meal and it is his taste for the fleshpots (as well as the hope of time for research) that makes the aristocratic largesse of Florence seem more appealing to him than canny, commercial Venice. In scene 9 his subtle tasting notes as he commends his old Sicilian wine to Ludovico and his indignation at the imputation that he might ever eat an olive without thinking show him to be a bon viveur. Laughton brought out the sensuality in Galileo clearly. With his ponderous girth and his shrewd eyes set above his thick lips and heavy jowls, he gave him an inimitable combination of gross coarseness and intellectual penetration. Brecht records in his notes:

> . . . it was just this mixture of the physical and the intellectual that attracted L. 'Galileo's physical contentment' at having his back rubbed by the boy is transformed into intellectual production . . . His sensual walking, the play of his hands in his pockets while he is planning new researches came close to being offensive. Whenever Galileo is creative, L. displayed a mixture of aggressiveness and defenceless softness and vulnerability.

Galileo's sensuality was accentuated in the American version of the play when it became a matter of undermining the figure's appeal for the audience. The Grand Inquisitor recognises in him a man of the flesh with no resistance to torture, and the Pope in scene 12 discerns a direct connection between Galileo's physical and intellectual appetites:

> THE POPE: . . . His thinking springs from sensuality. Give him an old wine or a new idea and he cannot say no.

Andrea's instinctive reaction when the Inquisition releases Galileo after his recantation is to sneer at his self-indulgence and so he calls him 'Wine pump! Snail eater!' As the character develops, Brecht tries to turn the appetites which reveal his earthy vitality and his common touch into selfish weaknesses which are of a piece with his avoidance of responsibility. The gourmet with the motto that 'pleasure takes some achieving' becomes a simple glutton.

Galileo is not the only character whom Brecht altered persistently in order to control the audience's perception of him; the same thing happened to Mother Courage and to Grusha in *The Caucasian Chalk Circle*. In both cases Brecht partially rewrote the roles to make the figures less sympathetic.

In the first nine scenes of the play Galileo is built up as a positive figure. His outline of the state of astronomy for Andrea in the expository opening scene reveals him as a passionate and lucid teacher as he expounds not only the principles of the Copernican system but also its social implications. He returns to these social implications in scene 8 in which he explains the Church's vested interest in the status quo to the Little Monk. He almost permits himself to criticise the plight of the peasants in his conversation with Bellarmin and Barberini, but his actual outburst against the landowners is reserved for Ludovico in scene 9. Galileo's analogy between the geocentric Ptolemaic system and the hierarchical rule of the feudal landowners, aided and abetted by the Church seems a natural one, but it is based on an Karl Marx's view of history as a class struggle, which was only formulated as a theory in the nineteenth century, so Brecht's Galileo looks at events around him with the benefit of considerable hindsight. In this respect he is in fact Brecht's spokesman, a twentieth century man, and if we bear this in mind his final revision of his self-estimate in the fourteenth scene may seem less implausible.

Galileo is a man of the people, at home with the workers in the Venice arsenal. He has, as has already been indicated, an acute understanding of the class structure of seventeenth century Italy, and he tells the Little Monk how applied science could improve the peasants' lot and change society. His assumption that he will sweep all before him in Florence, one of several miscalculations he makes in the play, is based on his faith in directness and plain speaking as much as on his newly acquired hard evidence. But his awareness of the role applied science might play takes second place to his overriding passion which is pure science. Pumps and proportional compasses are, like telescopes, 'kids stuff' and 'lucrative playthings', interesting only as a way of making money unless, like the telescope, they become research instruments. He must be aware of the telescope's potential military applications because the Procurator stresses this when he presents it to the Signoria, but he makes no comment on it.

In this phase of the play Galileo is essentially optimistic. His interpretation of his own situation is basically self-centred. He can see the weaknesses of the Venetian Republic because he feels exploited by it, but he overlooks the direr shortcomings of Florence because affluence seems to beckon from there. This and his naive faith in reason is enough to nullify Sagredo's warning and prevents him from seeeing the obvious, namely how little the Florentine state will welcome his discoveries.

The audience is on Galileo's side when he is confronted by the immovable, supercilious Florentine 'tuis' (to borrow the name Brecht coined for collaborative careerist intellectuals in his play *Turandot, or the Whitewashers' Congress*). It is on his side when he is exposed to the ribaldry of the assembled churchmen at the Collegium Romanum, and his modest response to Clavius's corroboration of his findings adds to his appeal. The audience is still on his side, though too well aware of what is coming to share his total bewilderment when, after their suave little debate, Cardinals Bellarmin and Barberini inform him that the work of Copernicus has been put on the Index. In the scene with the Little Monk his analysis of the social mechanisms that keep the rich rich and reconcile the poor to their poverty shows that his heart is in the right place, and the discovery in the sunspots scene that he has secretly been pursuing forbidden investigations continues to build up a positive figure.

All this means that when it comes to the exchange with Vanni in scene 11, it is difficult for an audience to see Galileo as a villain — which is what Brecht wants, for he sees Vanni's offer as Galileo's chance to commit himself to social progress, and his failure to accept it as social treachery. Brecht viewed Giordano Bruno as a lone voice in his times who could have recanted without damaging the cause of progress: not so Galileo:

In Bruno's time the battle was still a feeble one. But time does not stand still: a new class, the bourgeoisie with its new industries, has assertively entered the scene; no longer was it only scientific achievements that were at stake, but battles for their large-scale general exploitation.

When Vanni offers Galileo a lift, according to the view of the situation which Brecht expresses here, he is actually giving him a chance to participate in the exploitation of his own work for the benefit of humanity. But at this point in the play Galileo is waiting to hand over his latest book to the Grand Duke. He has sensed that something is wrong and has had transport waiting to smuggle him out of town if the need arises, so the audience is likely to put Galileo's tetchy dismissal of Vanni down to nerves in a tense situation and leave it at that.

Brecht inserted the figure of Vanni to represent the north Italian manufacturers, a faction so powerful that the Inquisitor in the next scene says they must be allowed to use Galileo's star charts, even though the theory on which they are based is heretical. The bourgeois capitalist manufacturers were in the end to replace the landowning aristocracy as the ruling class, but this was not apparent in the seventeenth century. Brecht's description of Laughton in the Vanni scene shows how serious he was about Galileo's 'historic decision':

> The actor Laughton showed Galileo in a state of great inner agitation during his talk with the ironfounder. He played it as a moment of decision — the wrong one.

It is straining credibility to suggest that the audience should be aware, far less that Galileo should know that his casual conversational gambit is in fact an historic decision. In his final conversation with Andrea, Galileo reflects that he was at this point so powerful that he could have defied the Inquisition, but it is difficult to take this seriously. The carnival scene demonstrates Galileo's popular effect and support, but nowhere in the play does Brecht demonstrate that the machinery of the state was incapable of dealing with the situation. The Grand Inquisitor seems fully in control, and the likelihood that Galileo could have defied him on his own ground and survived is nowhere established. Indeed the fact that the Church as the ideological arm of the state is so clearly the effective opponent of progress throughout the play makes it very difficult to focus on Galileo as the real enemy at the end.

The major changes in the final version of the play affected scene 14 where Brecht rewrote Galileo's lines extensively to prevent the audience from viewing him as a tragic victim of historical circumstances. He presents Galileo's clandestine experiments as a secret vice:

His appetite for knowledge feels to him like the impetus that makes him twitch. Scholarly activity, for him, is a sin: mortally dangerous, but impossible to do without. He has a fanatical hatred for humanity.

This is not entirely convincing. Galileo may be cynical and disillusioned; within the play his attitude to science travels the same course as Brecht's between the thirties and the fifties. It might be possible to view his scientific activity as a kind of covert self-gratification were it not for the secret copy of his treatise. A man whose only preoccupation is his own comfort does not ruin his eyesight by writing at night, nor does he risk discovery and even greater discomfort. If he makes a copy of a work which is being confiscated by the authorities as it progresses, there must at the back of his mind be the thought of transmitting the work to the outside world. This is not consistent with hatred of humanity. By the time he hands over the *Discorsi* to Andrea Galileo is a grey and bowed old man. The first visible change in his appearance is effected by the Inquisition in scene 13. Before his interrogation his characteristic stance is pugnacious, 'hands on his hams, thrust out tummy', but after twenty four days in custody he is almost unrecognisable. The audience is bound to see him here as a man who has been broken under duress, but Brecht is intent on overriding the obvious as his comment on Laughton's handling of the episode shows:

> The change L. selected was, as the playwright intended, not of a physical nature. There was something infantile, bed-wetting in his shambling gait, his grin, indicating a self-release of the lowest order, as if restraints had been thrown off that had been very necessary.

An actor can only indicate a change in his part by physical means, and the audience, which has only the physical characterisation to go on, is bound to ascribe Galileo's sudden decrepitude to his ordeal, and not to a hitherto studiously concealed character flaw. It will measure Galileo's self denigration against what it sees, which is not so much a clear-cut case of the scientist betraying his social responsibilities, more the professional dilemma of the modern scientist.

Galileo risks his well-being earlier, in the plague scene, partly because he is a compulsive researcher, partly because he needs proof at that stage to face his powerful enemies, and it is part of a consistent pattern of behaviour when he does it again in the fourteenth scene.

The figure that emerges is an ambivalent one, not the unmistakeable symbolic traitor Brecht strove for in trying to make Galileo the scapegoat for the development of the atom bomb. Ernst Busch who played Galileo at the Berliner Ensemble could not bring himself to accept Brecht's final reading of Galileo's character. He told him so and in the course of rehearsals after Brecht's death he imposed his own less critical interpretation on the character. He was not an intellectual type of actor, but he made the character work on the stage, though not along the lines Brecht had laid down. The theatre assimilated the text, and one reviewer recorded the following impression.

> What do I see on the stage during this intellectual exchange (in scene 14)? A man who has ruined his eyes at the telescope and almost gone blind by working in the light of the moon — making an illegal copy of a manuscript that will benefit mankind. We are not told this — we see it. . . . And I am supposed to hate this man? Condemn him? I can't, no matter how many commentaries they offer me. Not while I am watching it, not in the theatre. Reading is another matter.

The contradiction between Brecht's intention and his achievement is not a fault, certainly not in the theatre, and the character he created is richer in poetic possibilities than that his obsessively restricted view of it admitted.

Minor characters

Andrea grows up under Galileo's tutelage and absorbs his unqualified enthusiasm for science. His father is never mentioned in the play. Galileo's attachment to Andrea, in contrast to his disregard for Virginia, and the candidness and intimacy of Galileo's relationship with Mrs Sarti, not to speak of her devotion to him as seen in the plague scene, all seem to point to his being Galileo's son, though Brecht, himself no stranger to complicated family relationships, never says so explicitly. His responses are direct rather than thoughtful and he switches instantly from hero-worship to violent contempt when Galileo lets him down by recanting. It is he, when he is given the *Discorsi*, who interprets Galileo's recantation in retrospect as a cunning stratagem to protect the interests of science, which then prompts Galileo's self-denunciation in scene 14. His faith in science is unshaken to the end, and he departs for Holland as, in Galileo's terms, the first 'inventive dwarf'. The final scene at the border however shows him as a positive exponent of the cunning for survival that was the theme of the first version of the play.

The Little Monk only really has one scene. He experiences the contradiction between the attractions of the new science and the pastoral role of the church as a crisis of conscience, but this historically important theme is not developed since he is only there to give Galileo an opportunity to point out the connections between the Ptolemaic system, the established ideology and the oppression of the peasants.

Mrs Sarti, with her feet firmly on the ground, serves as a foil for Galileo in the first half of the play. She has to see that the household bills are paid, and they have a close relationship which enables her to scold him like a child and him to ignore her scolding. It is in some ways curious that there is no overtly sexual element in all this, and it is tempting to see the pointedly matter-of-fact words of the exchange when she decides to stay in the plague city to minister to his needs as the mask for something deeper.

Though Virginia is not her daughter as she clearly states in scene 9, it is Mrs Sarti who exposes the ruthlessness of Galileo's attitude in the same scene when he attacks Virginia's fiancé's ulterior motives as a landowner without any consideration of the effect on his daughter's future.

Mrs Sarti has no time for the new-fangled theories with which Galileo is filling her son's head in the first scene, and she has a superstitious faith in astrology, which Virginia shares. Although she shows no sign of excessive devoutness, she regards Galileo quite conventionally as a heretic. She disappears at the end of scene 9 when Andrea has grown up and Virginia takes over her functions in the household. In her last two speeches she addresses Galileo familiarly (German signals this more clearly); she has known all along that he has been conducting clandestine studies in proscribed areas and has kept quiet, but now she feels compelled to speak out:

> . . . If I choose to forfeit eternal bliss by sticking with a heretic that's my business, but you have no right to trample all over your daughter's happiness with your great feet.

Mrs Sarti is able to behave according to her personal lights and represents a commonsense attitude which cuts across ideology. She can consort with a heretic and still be a believing catholic. Her healthy pragmatism is seen in a slightly comic light before the Florentine court arrives to view Galileo's telescope, when she says *she* would have softened them up with a good dinner. Galileo himself uses Mrs Sarti in scene 3 to prove to Sagredo that the common people are avid for the truth, a striking irony, since she is in fact incorrigibly conservative and indifferent to his discoveries. She seems, in contrast to the class-conscious folk in the carnival scene, to be an apolitical individualist, who like Kragler in *Drums in the Night* in the final estimate goes her own way.

Virginia had more spirit in the first version of the play where she sent Ludovico packing herself in scene 9 because of his qualms about Galileo's interest in sunspots. In the final version, as part of Brecht's efforts to detach the audience's sympathies from Galileo, the latter puts paid to her marriage while she is offstage. His behaviour towards her deprives her of a life of her own. In the third scene, in contrast to his interest in educating Andrea, he refuses to let her look through the telescope, and Brecht in his notes suggests that it is slights like this which turn her into the agent of the Inquisition. Like Mrs Sarti, she never sheds her conservative disbelief in Galileo's new universe, but unlike Mrs Sarti whom she replaces in the second half of the play, she is bent on saving Galileo's soul and ends up an old maid spying for the Inquisition. She is not alterable nor able to alter, as are the key figures and target audience in Brecht's epic theatre.

Barberini in the play as in history is an amateur scientist and well disposed towards Galileo, which causes Galileo to miscalculate gravely on his attitude to Copernican research when he becomes Pope. The scene in which his investment with his robes of office becomes a visual demonstration of how official policy replaces his private views is a classic example of the way 'social being determines thought' in epic theatre. This kind of character change had interested Brecht since the dismantling and reassembly of Galy Gay in *Man equals Man*.

Vanni is a new character in the final version of the play, replacing Matti, who though an ironfounder, was merely an importunate incidental figure in the Laughton version. He represents the rising manufacturing classes who want Galileo on their side. His offer of help supports Galileo's later unhistorical and not quite plausible claim that at the time of his recantation he was strong enough to stand up to the inquisition. Brecht intends Galileo's rejection of his offer to be the point at which Galileo turns into an antisocial figure.

Ludovico is the representative of the land-owning class. He is an ironic observer of Galileo's fraud with the telescope at the beginning of the play. In his last scene he puts the case for the landowners who depend on a docile peasantry for their labour, a relationship which Galileo's scientific discoveries could destabilize. His status demands that his marriage be impeccably conventional. Galileo's rude provocation which prompts Ludovico to break off his engagement would be a laudable gesture, if it were not a purely private one, selfishly made without a thought for the disastrous consequences for his daughter.

Epic theatre

The literary term 'epic' is traditionally applied to forms of writing in which the author recounts a story, using as many episodes and characters as a comprehensive account of his subject demands. In modern times the epic has been the preserve of prose fiction, and its standard form the novel. The term 'dramatic' is traditionally applied to forms of writing intended for performance, and these are limited in number of characters and settings by the conventions and resources of the theatre, and in length by the audience's patience and concentration, so that dramatists are in practice restricted to presenting a concentrated plot which shows a conflict and its resolution. The term 'epic theatre', which was first used in Germany in the 1920's and has become firmly associated with the name of Brecht, though the work of his friend Erwin Piscator, for whose 'Political Theatre' at the Nollendorfplatz in Berlin he occasionally worked in 1927-28, pioneered some of its techniques. Epic theatre cuts across the traditional divisions. Epic story-telling is objective; the author stands back from his story as he tells it, and he may interpolate his own comment on events. It was the objectivity and the simultaneous scope for comment in epic writing that attracted the dramatist Brecht, and the beginning of epic theatre coincided with German experiments in the use of the theatre as an instrument of political instruction.

From the beginning of his career Brecht had fought a running battle against the conventional theatre of his day which he dismissed as 'culinary', since, like expert cooking, it delighted the senses without impinging on the mind. Banners in the auditorium for the production of one of his first plays, *Drums in the Night* in 1922, told the audience not to 'gawp so romantically', and in his essay *On Experimental Theatre* (1939) Brecht asked,

> How can the theatre be entertaining and at the same time instructive? How can it be taken out of the traffic in intellectual drugs and transformed from a place of illusion to a place of insight?

For Brecht the traditional, or dramatic theatre was a place where the audience were absorbed into a comforting illusion which played on their emotions and left them drained, but with a sense of satisfaction which predisposed them to accept the world as they found it. What he himself was looking for was a theatre that would help to change the world.

He first tabulated his ideas on epic theatre in his *Notes on the Opera 'The Rise and Fall of the City of Mahagonny'* (1930) where he set out the contrasts between the dramatic theatre and the epic theatre in a list.

DRAMATIC THEATRE	EPIC THEATRE
plot	narrative
implicates the spectator in a stage situation	turns the spectator into an observer, but
wears down his capacity for action	arouses his capacity for action
provides him with sensations	forces him to take decisions
experience	picture of the world
the spectator is involved in something	he is made to face something
suggestion	argument
instinctive feelings are preserved	brought to the point of recognition
the spectator is in the thick of it, shares the experience	the spectator stands outside, studies
the human being is taken for granted	the human being is the object the inquiry
he is unalterable	he is alterable and able to alter
eyes on the finish	eyes on the course
one scene makes another	each scene for itself
growth	montage
linear development	in curves
evolutionary determinism	jumps
man as a fixed point	man as a process
thought determines being	social being determines thought
feeling	reason

(from *Brecht on Theatre*, 9. 37)

The first change of emphasis Brecht advocated was in the manner in which events were presented to the audience. Dramatic theatre enacted plots, involved the audience and stimulated their emotions only to dissipate this active response. Epic theatre was to tell a story in a way that invited the audience to consider the events involved and then to make their own assessment of them. To achieve this, adjustments had to be made to the form of the play. The dramatic play was a closed system of interdependent scenes, each one evolving inexorably from its predecessor, but with the plot so structured that the audience was kept in suspense, wondering how it would all end. The epic play was to be assembled as a montage of independent incidents which showed a process taking place; it would move from scene to scene by curves and jumps, which would keep the audience alert to the way in which things were happening, so that they would finally be able, would indeed be compelled, to judge whether that was the right way. Brecht sometimes compared his plays to scientific experiments; specimens of human behaviour were subjected to scrutiny to see what principles governed them and whether these principles could be improved. Change for the better lay at the centre of Brecht's thinking, and this meant altering the classical notion that the hero of a play should be a fixed character. The conflict between such immutable 'Characters' and their world was the stuff of traditional drama, but Brecht rejected the notion that human nature was fixed, and that man's own thinking governed his being, in favour of a concept of human nature as capable of change. In epic theatre man's thinking is conditioned by his social situation and will change if that changes. At the same time he is the agent of social change, so that there is a constant dialectic, or process of reciprocal influence and change.

No one would call *Life of Galileo* a classic example of epic theatre. Brecht himself evaluated it in his diary as

> . . . . technically a step backwards, too opportunistic, like *Senora Carrar's Rifles*. One would have to rewrite the play completely to capture the 'breeze which blows from new coasts', the rosy dawn of science. everything would have to be more direct, without the interiors, the 'atmosphere', the empathy. everything would have to be more of a planetary demonstration. (25.2.39)

Senora Carrar's Rifles (1937) was a short, conventional, naturalistic play, which was conceived as a propaganda piece for the Republic during the Spanish Civil War. Brecht had taken a more positive view of *Life of Galileo* three months earlier.

> *Life of Galileo* completed. it took three weeks. the only problems arose with the final scene. as in ST JOAN it needed one artistic touch at the end to make sure the audience kept the necessary detachment. even the most vacuous empathiser must at least now, via his own empathy with Galileo, be aware of the alienation effect. with strict epic presentation a permissible form of empathy occurs. (23.11.38)

Both comments relate to the first version of the play, and in both cases Brecht was satisfied with the character of Galileo and with the selection of historical incidents, but his later response identifies an excess of general empathy and atmosphere, and too little feeling of historical change. Any remedy would require to be arrived at by trial and error on stage and would aim to make the play more of a 'planetary demonstration'. In *The Messingkauf Dialogues* the theatre is divided into the P and K types. In the P-type the viewer sits back as if in a planetarium and watches an ingenious quasi-mechanical simulation of the movements of man in society. P-type theatre is critical, realistic and broadly synonymous with epic theatre.

Life of Galileo, although it covers twenty-six years and leaves long gaps as it traces Galileo's tussle with the Papacy, uses conventional techniques of dramatic concentration rather than epic curves and jumps. Galileo's work on sunspots and floating bodies is postdated by ten years to make it coincide with the accession of the new Pope for dramatic effect, and several scenes, most strikingly scene 11 when Galileo is summoned by the Inquisition, end with curtain effects. The action moves from Padua to Venice, Florence, Rome, then back to the vicinity of Florence and on to the Italian border, but there is no loose-knit rambling action, no real sense of movement, no need for the revolving stage which gave *Mother Courage and her Children* and *The Caucasian Chalk Circle* their characteristic epic openness. *Life of Galileo* is an indoor play, with the exception of the carnival and border scenes. The carnival scene has the only song in the play (apart from Lorenzo de Medici's poem which is sung in the background in scene 7), and the border scene is an epilogue. It opens up new perspectives of a future for science in freedom and must be construed as a comment on the preceding action. It is, however, mostly omitted in production. There is no commentator in the play, and the characters never step out of their roles and never have their feelings expressed through a third party. Formally almost the only device from his standard epic repertoire that Brecht uses are the captions and verse summaries that he places at the beginning of the scenes as anti-illusionistic devices to eliminate suspense. There is however one visual device that is peculiar to this play. The principles of the Ptolemaic and Copernican systems are the premises on which intellectual structure of the play stands, and they must be clarified for the audience at the outset. Brecht does this in terms a child can understand, and he does it with images as much as words. The epic demonstrations of the revolution of the earth with a chair and a washstand, and of its rotation with an apple and a splinter of wood in scene 1 are theatrical inventions of the first order, and they set a pattern of visible experiment which runs through the play.

Leaving form aside, there is a fundamental sense in which the principles of epic theatre are internalised in the thematic conflict between scientific rationalism and dogmatic obscurantism. Galileo represents the principle of constructive analysis. He tells Andrea in the sunspots scene that when they have found what they are looking for they will regard it with particular mistrust, and only when all alternatives have been eliminated will they accept it. This radical doubt in the face of the physical world has its equivalent in the dramatist Brecht's alienation or estrangement of the social world with a view to identifying antisocial forms of behaviour, so that they can be eliminated. Epic drama and Galilean science both aim to initiate social change. On the other side of the equation dramatic theatre is based on Aristotle's aesthetics, and, as Brecht interpreted it, its effect was to dissipate the audience's responses and predispose them to accept things as they are, just as the reactionary aim of Church policy in the play is to absorb and transform discontent and preserve the status quo. The Church derives its theoretical justification from the writings of Aristotle, and it uses the Scriptures as opiates to dull the sufferings of the peasantry.

In the end, the disparity between the scientific advances of Galileo's time and the hidebound social structures that prevented their being exploited for the general benefit would have left the audience with clear-cut questions about the nature of society had not Brecht elected to complicate the issue by undermining the position of the scientist too.

Language

Language in *Life of Galileo* varies with character. Galileo strikes a scientific and logical tone in the first scene when he insists that Andrea use the geometrical formulation 'describe a circle' rather than just 'make a circle', and he sustains this tone throughout. Even his aphorisms, of which the pithiest is, 'The sum of the angles in a triangle cannot be varied to suit the Vatican's convenience' are scientific. When, in his 'Welcome to the gutter' speech in scene 14 he uses figurative language it is intentionally striking, to lend force to his self-condemnation. By contrast the Procurator's language is occasionally flowery, while that of the Florentine Mathematician and Philosopher is teasingly precious and ironic. Galileo's exchanges with Andrea and Mrs Sarti are direct and laconic, but he can rise to a formal exchange and swap Biblical quotations with Barberini and Bellarmin who have their own carefully formulated, detached upper-class tone. Vanni introduces the vocabulary of manufacturing industry into the play.

There are a number of literary references, and, besides the Bible, the play quotes Dante, Voltaire and Einstein and incorporates lines from Horace and Lorenzo de Medici.

The script that Laughton produced with Brecht was shorter and more terse than any of the German versions. Where the present translation, following the final German version faithfully, has:

> LUDOVICO: I happened to be in the area, inspecting our vineyards at Buccioli, and couldn't resist the chance. (p. 75)

Laughton has:

> LUDOVICO: I decided on the spur of the moment. I was over inspecting our vineyards at Bucciole. I couldn't keep away.

Staging

For the American production Brecht and Laughton established certain guidelines for the design. The sets were not to suggest to the spectators that they were in a real room, but show 'in an imaginative and artistically pleasing way' the general historical setting. Props (including doors) and furniture were to be solidly realistic and 'above all of social and historical interest'. Costumes were to be individualised and to look worn. Social differences which are difficult to distinguish in period costume were to be emphasised.

The Berliner Ensemble production was designed by Caspar

Neher. He enclosed the stage in a high, open, neutral box set which
had several flush doors in the back and sides for entrances and
exits. The walls were clad in copper sheeting which comes up
rather dark in photographs. John Willett found it too opulent when
he saw it, and the costumes did not show up well against it. There
was paving on the floor. The use of a neutral space which could be
transformed for each scene by a few props or parts of buildings
was pioneered in Germany after the Great War by the Expressionists,
and Brecht adopted it as a way of combating illusion in his epic
theatre and reminding his audience that it was not watching real
life, but a simulation of life. The props and pieces of scenery for
Life of Galileo were light and easy to erect and remove. The
costumes provided the only colour. The bareness of the stage
exposed the action in a cool, unatmospheric space which was
intended to counterbalance the relative lack of epic form in the
writing.

In the first scene an enlarged design for a fortification was used
as a backdrop to signify Galileo's work at the Venice arsenal.
Sparsely furnished with a bed, a chart on an easel, a washstand, a
table and an armillary sphere, the stage was not a specific room but
a summary of Galileo's living environment. His studies in and near
Florence were variations of this initial stage configuration.

The hall of the Collegium Romanum was indicated by a pair of
six-candle overhead chandeliers and three portals with panelled
doors, and the same set with a door opening at the back on to a
brightly lit painting served as Cardinal Bellarmin's house. Neither
place had any furnishings.

For the carnival scene the only prop was a fountain in the
middle of the stage, and the giant puppets and colourful revellers
gave the scene its visual impact.

The garden of the Florentine ambassador's house where Virginia
and Galileo's pupils hear his recantation was indicated by a small
circular fountain at the centre of the stage with four curved
benches disposed round it. Since time plays an important part in
the scene there was a giant golden sundial on the back wall.

The figures in the play moved in large empty spaces, and the
overall effect was one of restraint and economy. This type of bare
stage, relieved only by a few telling, solidly realistic props was a
powerful influence on staging in Britain after the Berliner
Ensemble's visit in 1956.

Meaning

The role of science and technology in the modern world has become progressively more ambivalent since Brecht's death. In the military field the debate on the issue has been fuelled by the superpowers' policies of nuclear deterrence, chemical warfare in Vietnam, the experimental development of biological weapons and latterly the projected deployment of weaponry in space. Even non-military applications of science have become suspect in recent years as evidence of their harmful effect on the environment has come to light, and West Germany now has a significant Green Party which articulates public hostility to the uncontrolled exploitation of nature by science, so the issue at the centre of *Life of Galileo* is vitally alive. Brecht's own interpretation of the play, which makes Galileo directly responsible over the centuries for the atom bomb and suggests that things would have been different if Galileo had entered into an alliance with the progressive middle classes now seems less convincing than it appeared to his critics and even some of his collaborators at the time of writing, but this does not weaken the play which remains the most searching examination of the ethics of science that has been written for the stage. Galileo's journey from bright optimism to despairing cynicism under the constraints of an authoritarian regime still has the power to move and audience, but it is the cynicism and despair that Brecht found so despicable which touch a contemporary nerve. Brecht's analysis simplifies the issue when it implies that Galileo could have changed the course of history by entering an alliance with progressive social forces. Scientific ethics in the U.S.S.R. are not noticeably different from those in the U.S.A. Yet Galileo's crisis of conscience and moral collapse, precisely because their presentation is contradictory, leave the audience with a problem and challenge them to relate it to contemporary experience in the best epic tradition.

Further reading

Bertolt Brecht: *Brecht on Theatre* (translation and notes by John
    Willett), Eyre Methuen, London, 1964. Brecht's essential
    theoretical and critical writings assembled in one handy volume.
Graham Bartram and Anthony Waine: *Brecht in Perspective*,
    Longman, London and New York, 1982. Essays by British
    scholars which examine Brecht's literary, historical and social
    background, relate him to the German theatrical tradition, and
    compare him with seminal figures like Piscator and Stanislavsky.
Keith A. Dickson: *Towards Utopia*, Oxford University Press, 1978.
    Closely argued study of Brecht and his work which draws on
    research in English, German and Russian. Dickson pursues the
    utopian vision behind Brecht's satirical presentation of life. The
    book is organized around themes (Man and Society, the
    Historical Perspective, etc.) and deals with plays, poetry and
    prose.
Martin Esslin: *Brecht: a Choice of Evils*, 4th Ed., Methuen, London,
    1984. An early appraisal with useful insights, in spite of the
    writer's obvious antipathy to Brecht's politics.
Claude Hill: *Bertolt Brecht*, Twayne, Boston, 1975. An American
    survey, clear and useful, with separate chapters on major works.
James K. Lyon: *Bertolt Brecht in America*, Methuen, London,
    1982. Fascinating account of Brecht's U.S. exile with three
    chapters on Brecht, Laughton and *Life of Galileo*.
Michael Morley: *Brecht, a Study*, Heinemann, London, 1977.
    A succinct survey of Brecht's work, including the poems, with
    the plays grouped in chapters according to theme or style.
    Life of Galileo comes under the heading, 'The Exceptional
    Individual'.
Jan Needle and Peter Thompson: *Brecht*, Blackwell, Oxford, 1981.
    The authors have studied Brecht in English translation. They are
    best on the plays in performance.
Alfred D. White: *Bertolt Brecht's Great Plays*, Macmillan, London,
    1978. Analyses of the major plays in separate chapters.
John Willett: *The Theatre of Bertolt Brecht*, 4th ed., Eye Methuen,
    London, 1977. Seminal compendium of basic information.

John Willett: *Brecht in Context*, Methuen, London, 1984. Looks at
    Brecht from several aspects such as politics, music, expressionism
    etc. Includes Willett's impressions of the original Berliner
    Ensemble production of *Galileo*.

All Brecht's major plays (and many minor works) are published in
English translation in the Methuen Modern Plays series. Also
published by Methuen are volumes of Brecht's *Poems 1913-56,
Short Stories 1921-46* and *Diaries 1920-22*.

Above: Scene 1. Galileo (Laughton) with Mrs Sarti and Andrea.
Below: end of Scene 9. Virginia in her wedding dress runs into
Galileo's study

Life of Galileo

Collaborator: M. STEFFIN

Translator: JOHN WILLETT

Characters

GALILEO GALILEI
ANDREA SARTI
MRS SARTI, *Galileo's housekeeper, Andrea's mother*
LUDOVICO MARSILI, *a rich young man*
THE PROCURATOR OF PADUA UNIVERSITY, *Mr Priuli*
SAGREDO, *Galileo's friend*
VIRGINIA, *Galileo's daughter*
FEDERZONI, *a lens-grinder, Galileo's assistant*
THE DOGE
SENATORS
COSIMO DE MEDICI, *Grand Duke of Florence*
THE COURT CHAMBERLAIN
THE THEOLOGIAN
THE PHILOSOPHER
THE MATHEMATICIAN
THE OLDER COURT LADY
THE YOUNGER COURT LADY
GRAND-DUCAL FOOTMAN
TWO NUNS
TWO SOLDIERS
THE OLD WOMAN
A FAT PRELATE
TWO SCHOLARS
TWO MONKS
TWO ASTRONOMERS
A VERY THIN MONK

THE VERY OLD CARDINAL
FATHER CHRISTOPHER CLAVIUS, *astronomer*
THE LITTLE MONK
THE CARDINAL INQUISITOR
CARDINAL BARBERINI, *subsequently Pope Urban VIII*
CARDINAL BELLARMIN
TWO CLERICAL SECRETARIES
TWO YOUNG LADIES
FILIPPO MUCIUS, *a scholar*
MR GAFFONE, *Rector of the University of Pisa*
THE BALLAD-SINGER
HIS WIFE
VANNI, *an ironfounder*
AN OFFICIAL
A HIGH OFFICIAL
AN INDIVIDUAL
A MONK
A PEASANT
A FRONTIER GUARD
A CLERK
Men, women, children

I

Galileo Galilei, a teacher of mathematics at Padua, sets out to prove Copernicus's new cosmogony

> In the year sixteen hundred and nine
> Science's light began to shine.
> At Padua city in a modest house
> Galileo Galilei set out to prove
> The sun is still, the earth is on the move.

Galileo's rather wretched study in Padua. It is morning. A boy, Andrea, the housekeeper's son, brings in a glass of milk and a roll.

GALILEO *washing down to the waist, puffing and cheerful*: Put that milk on the table, and don't you shut any of those books.

ANDREA: Mother says we must pay the milkman. Or he'll start making a circle round our house, Mr Galilei.

GALILEO: Describing a circle, you mean, Andrea.

ANDREA: Whichever you like. If we don't pay the bill he'll start describing a circle round us, Mr Galilei.

GALILEO: Whereas when Mr Cambione the bailiff comes straight for us what sort of distance between two points is he going to pick?

ANDREA *grinning*: The shortest.

GALILEO: Right. I've got something for you. Look behind the star charts.

Andrea rummages behind the star charts and brings out a big wooden model of the Ptolemaic system.

ANDREA: What is it?

GALILEO: That's an armillary sphere. It's a contraption to show how the planets move around the earth, according to our forefathers.

ANDREA: How?

GALILEO: Let's examine it. Start at the beginning. Description?

ANDREA: In the middle there's a small stone.

GALILEO: That's the earth.

ANDREA: Round it there are rings, one inside another.

GALILEO: How many?

ANDREA: Eight.

GALILEO: That's the crystal spheres.

ANDREA: Stuck to the rings are little balls.

GALILEO: The stars.

ANDREA: Then there are bands with words painted on them.

GALILEO: What sort of words?

ANDREA: Names of stars.

GALILEO: Such as . . .

ANDREA: The lowest ball is the moon, it says. Above that's the sun.

GALILEO: Now start the sun moving.

ANDREA *moves the rings*: That's great. But we're so shut in.

GALILEO *drying himself*: Yes, I felt that first time I saw one of those. We're not the only ones to feel it. *He tosses the towel to Andrea, for him to dry his back with.* Walls and spheres and immobility! For two thousand years people have believed that the sun and all the stars of heaven rotate around mankind. Pope, cardinals, princes, professors, captains, merchants, fishwives and schoolkids thought they were sitting motionless inside this crystal sphere. But now we are breaking out of it, Andrea, at full speed. Because the old days are over and this is a new time. For the last hundred years mankind has seemed to be expecting something.

Our cities are cramped, and so are men's minds. Superstition and the plague. But now the word is 'that's how things are, but they won't stay like that'. Because everything is in motion, my friend.

I like to think that it began with the ships. As far as men could remember they had always hugged the coast, then suddenly they abandoned the coast line and ventured out across the seas. On our old continent a rumour sprang up: there might be new ones. And since our ships began sailing to them the laughing continents have got the message: the great ocean they feared, is a little puddle. And a vast desire has sprung up to know the reasons for everything: why a stone falls when you let it go and why it rises when you toss it up. Each day something fresh is discovered. Men of a hundred, even, are getting the young people to bawl the latest example into their ear. There have been a lot of discoveries, but there is still plenty to be found out. So future generations should have enough to do.

As a young man in Siena I watched a group of building workers argue for five minutes, then abandon a thousand-year old method of shifting granite blocks in favour of a new and more efficient arrangement of the ropes. Then and there I knew, the old days are over and this is a new time. Soon humanity is going to understand its abode, the heavenly body on which it dwells. What is written in the old books is no longer good enough. For where faith has been enthroned for a thousand years doubt now sits. Everyone says: right, that's what it says in the books, but let's have a look for ourselves. That most solemn truths are being familiarly nudged; what was never doubted before is doubted now.

This has created a draught which is blowing up the gold-embroidered skirts of the prelates and princes, revealing the fat and skinny legs underneath, legs like our own. The heavens, it turns out, are empty. Cheerful laughter is our response. But the waters of the earth drive the new spinning machines, while in the shipyards, the ropewalks and sail-lofts five hundred hands are moving together in a new system.

It is my prophecy that our own lifetime will see astronomy being discussed in the marketplaces. Even the fishwives' sons will hasten off to school. For these novelty-seeking people in our cities will be delighted with a new astronomy that sets the earth moving too. The old idea was always that the stars were fixed to a crystal vault to stop them falling down. Today we have found the courage to let them soar through space without support; and they are travelling at full speed just like our ships, at full speed and without support.

And the earth is rolling cheerfully around the sun, and the fishwives, merchants, princes, cardinals and even the Pope are rolling with it.

The universe has lost its centre overnight, and woken up to find it has countless centres. So that each one can now be seen as the centre, or none at all. Suddenly there is a lot of room.

Our ships sail far overseas, our planets move far out into space, in chess too the rooks have begun sweeping far across the board.

What does the poet say? O early morning of beginnings . . .

ANDREA:

O early morning of beginnings
O breath of wind that
Cometh from new shores!

And you'd better drink up your milk, because people are sure to start arriving soon.

GALILEO: Have you understood what I told you yesterday?

ANDREA: What? All that about Copper Knickers and turning?

GALILEO: Yes.

ANDREA: No. What d'you want me to understand that for? It's very difficult, and I'm not even eleven till October.

GALILEO: I particularly want you to understand it. Getting

people to understand it is the reason why I go on working
and buying expensive books instead of paying the milkman.

ANDREA: But I can see with my own eyes that the sun goes
down in a different place from where it rises. So how can it
stay still? Of course it can't.

GALILEO: You can see, indeed! What can you see? Nothing
at all. You just gawp. Gawping isn't seeing. *He puts the iron
washstand in the middle of the room.* Right: this is the sun. Sit
down. *Andrea sits on one of the chairs, Galileo stands behind him.*
Where's the sun, right or left of you?

ANDREA: Left.

GALILEO: And how does it get to be on your right?

ANDREA: By you carrying it to my right, of course.

GALILEO: Isn't there any other way? *He picks him up along
with the chair and makes an about-turn.* Now where's the
sun?

ANDREA: On my right.

GALILEO: Did it move?

ANDREA: Not really.

GALILEO: So what did move?

ANDREA: Me.

GALILEO *bellows*: Wrong! You idiot! The chair!

ANDREA: But me with it!

GALILEO: Of course. The chair's the earth. You're sitting on
it.

MRS SARTI *has entered in order to make the bed. She has been
watching*: Just what are you up to with my boy, Mr Galilei?

GALILEO: Teaching him to see, Mrs Sarti.

MRS SARTI: What, by lugging him round the room?

ANDREA: Lay off, mother. You don't understand.

MRS SARTI: Oh, don't I? And you do: is that it? There's a
young gentleman wants some lessons. Very well dressed,
got a letter of introduction too. *Hands it over.* You'll have
Andrea believing two and two makes five any minute now,
Mr Galilei. As if he didn't already muddle up everything

you tell him. Only last night he was arguing that the earth goes round the sun. He's got it into his head that some gentleman called Copper Knickers worked that one out.

ANDREA: Didn't Copper Knickers work it out, Mr Galilei? You tell her.

MRS SARTI: You surely can't tell him such stories? Making him trot it all out at school so the priests come and see me because he keeps on coming out with blasphemies. You should be ashamed of yourself, Mr Galilei.

GALILEO *eating his breakfast*: In consequence of our researches, Mrs Sarti, and as a result of intensive argument, Andrea and I have made discoveries which we can no longer hold back from the world. A new time has begun, a time it's a pleasure to live in.

MRS SARTI: Well. Let's hope your new time will allow us to pay the milkman, Mr Galilei. *Indicating the letter of introduction.* Just do me a favour and don't send this man away. I'm thinking of the milk bill. *Exit.*

GALILEO *laughing*: Let me at least finish my milk! *To Andrea*: So you did understand something yesterday?

ANDREA: I only told her to wake her up a bit. But it isn't true. All you did with me and that chair was turn it sideways, not like this. *He makes a looping motion with his arm.* Or I'd have fallen off, and that's a fact. Why didn't you turn the chair over? Because it would have proved I'd fall off if you turned it that way. So there.

GALILEO: Look, I proved to you . . .

ANDREA: But last night I realised that if the earth turned that way I'd be hanging head downwards every night, and that's a fact.

GALILEO *takes an apple from the table*: Right, now this is the earth.

ANDREA: Don't keep on taking that sort of example, Mr Galilei. They always work.

GALILEO *putting back the apple*: Very well.

ANDREA: Examples always work if you're clever. Only I can't lug my mother round in a chair like you did me. So you see it's a rotten example really. And suppose your apple is the earth like you say? Nothing follows.

GALILEO *laughing*: You just don't want to know.

ANDREA: Pick it up again. Why don't I hang head downwards at night, then?

GALILEO: Right: here's the earth and here's you standing on it. *He takes a splinter from a piece of firewood and sticks it into the apple.* Now the earth's turning round.

ANDREA: And now I'm hanging head downwards.

GALILEO: What d'you mean? Look at it carefully. Where's your head?

ANDREA *pointing*: There. Underneath.

GALILEO: Really? *He turns it back*: Isn't it in precisely the same position? Aren't your feet still underneath? You don't stand like this when I turn it, do you? *He takes out the splinter and puts it in upside down.*

ANDREA: No. Then why don't I notice it's turning?

GALILEO: Because you're turning with it. You and the air above you and everything else on this ball.

ANDREA: Then why does it look as if the sun's moving?

GALILEO *turns the apple and the splinter round again*: Right: you're seeing the earth below you; that doesn't change, it's always underneath you and so far as you're concerned it doesn't move. But then look what's above you. At present the lamp's over your head, but once I've turned the apple what's over it now; what's above?

ANDREA *turns his head similarly*: The stove.

GALILEO: And where's the lamp?

ANDREA: Underneath.

GALILEO: Ha.

ANDREA: That's great: that'll give her something to think about. *Enter Ludovico Marsili, a rich young man.*

GALILEO: This place is getting like a pigeon loft.

LUDOVICO: Good morning, sir. My name is Ludovico Marsili.

GALILEO *reading his letter of introduction*: So you've been in Holland?

LUDOVICO: Where they were all speaking about you, Mr Galilei.

GALILEO: Your family owns estates in the Campagna?

LUDOVICO: Mother wanted me to have a look-see, find out what's cooking in the world and all that.

GALILEO: And in Holland they told you that in Italy, for instance, I was cooking?

LUDOVICO: And since Mother also wanted me to have a look-see in the sciences . . .

GALILEO: Private tuition: ten scudi a month.

LUDOVICO: Very well, sir.

GALILEO: What are your main interests?

LUDOVICO: Horses.

GALILEO: Ha.

LUDOVICO: I've not got the brains for science, Mr Galilei.

GALILEO: Ha. In that case we'll make it fifteen scudi a month.

LUDOVICO: Very well, Mr Galilei.

GALILEO: I'll have to take you first thing in the morning. That'll be your loss, Andrea. You'll have to drop out of course. You don't pay, see?

ANDREA: I'm off. Can I have the apple?

GALILEO: Yes.

Exit Andrea.

LUDOVICO: You'll have to be patient with me. You see, everything in the sciences goes against a fellow's good sound commonsense. I mean, look at that queer tube thing they're selling in Amsterdam. I gave it a good looking-over. A green leather casing and a couple of lenses, one this way – *he indicates a concave lens* – and the other that way – *he indicates a convex lens*. One of them's supposed to magnify and the other reduces. Anyone in his right mind would expect them to cancel out. They don't. The thing makes everything appear five times the size. That's science for you.

GALILEO: What appears five time the size?

LUDOVOCI: Church spires, pigeons, anything that's a long way off.

GALILEO: Did you yourself see church spires magnified in this way?

LUDOVICO: Yes sir.

GALILEO: And this tube has two lenses? *He makes a sketch on a piece of paper.* Did it look like that? *Ludovico nods.* How old's this invention?

LUDOVICO: Not more than a couple of days, I'd say, when I left Holland; at least that's how long it had been on the market.

GALILEO *almost friendly*: And why does it have to be physics? Why not horsebreeding?

Enter Mrs Sarti unobserved by Galileo.

LUDOVOCI: Mother thinks you can't do without a bit of science. Nobody can drink a glass of wine without science these days, you know.

GALILEO: Why didn't you pick a dead language or theology? That's easier. *Sees Mrs Sarti.* Right, come along on Tuesday morning. *Ludovico leaves.*

GALILEO: Don't give me that look. I accepted him.

MRS SARTI: Because I caught your eye in time. The procurrator of the university is out there.

GALILEO: Show him in, he matters. There may be 500 scudi in this. I wouldn't have to bother with pupils.

Mrs Sarti shows in the procurator. Galileo has finished dressing, meanwhile jotting down figures on a piece of paper.

GALILEO: Good morning. Lend us half a scudo. *The procurator digs a coin out of his purse and Galileo gives it to Sarti.* Sarti, tell Andrea to go to the spectacle-maker's and get two lenses: there's the prescription.

Exit Mrs Sarti with the paper.

PROCURATOR: I have come in connection with your application for a rise in salary to 1000 scudi. I regret that I cannot recommend it to the university. As you know, courses in mathematics do not attract new students. Mathematics, so to speak, is an unproductive art. Not that our Republic doesn't esteem it most highly. It may not be so essential as philosophy or so useful as theology, but it nonetheless offers infinite pleasures to its adepts.

GALILEO *busy with his papers*: My dear fellow, I can't manage on 500 scudi.

PROCURATOR: But, Mr Galilei, your week consists of two two-hour lectures. Given your outstanding reputation you can certainly get plenty of pupils who can afford private lessons. Haven't you got private pupils?

GALILEO: Too many, sir. I teach and I teach, and when am I supposed to learn? God help us, I'm not half as sharp as those gentlemen in the philosophy department. I'm stupid. I understand absolutely nothing. So I'm compelled to fill the gaps in my knowledge. And when am I supposed to do that? When am I to get on with my research? Sir, my branch of knowledge is still avid to know. The greatest problems still find us with nothing but hypotheses to go on. Yet we keep asking ourselves for proofs. How am I to provide them if I can only maintain my home by having to take any thickhead who can afford the money and din it into him that parallel lines meet at infinity?

PROCURATOR: Don't forget that even if the Republic pays less well than certain princes it does guarantee freedom of research. In Padua we even admit Protestants to our lectures. And give them doctors' degrees too. In Mr Cremonini's case we not only failed to hand him over to the Inquisition when he was proved, proved, Mr Galilei – to have made irreligious remarks, but actually granted him a rise in salary. As far as Holland Venice is known as the republic where the Inquisition has no say. That should mean something to you, being an astronomer, that's to say operating in a field where for some time now the doctrines of the church have hardly been treated with proper respect.

GALILEO: You people handed Mr Giordano Bruno over to Rome. Because he was propagating the ideas of Copernicus.

PROCURATOR: Not because he was propagating the ideas of Mr Copernicus, which anyway are wrong, but because he was not a Venetian citizen and had no regular position here. So you needn't drag in the man they burned. Incidentally, however free we are, I wouldn't go around openly citing a name like his, which is subject to the express anathema of the church: not even here, not even here.

GALILEO: Your protection of freedom of thought is pretty good business, isn't it? By showing how everywhere else the Inquisition prevails and burns people, you get good teachers cheap for this place. You make up for your attitude to the Inquisition by paying lower salaries than anyone.

PROCURATOR: That's most unfair. What use would it be to you to have limitless spare time for research if any ignorant monk in the Inquisition could just put a ban on your thoughts? Every rose has its thorn, Mr Galilei, and every ruler has his monks.

GALILEO: So what's the good of free research without free time to research in? What happens to its results? Perhaps you'd kindly show this paper about falling bodies to the gentlemen at the Signoria – *he indicates a bundle of manuscript* – and ask them if it isn't worth a few extra scudi.

PROCURATOR: It's worth infinitely more than that, Mr Galilei.

GALILEO: Sir, not infinitely more, a mere 500 scudi more.

PROCURATOR: What is worth scudi is what brings scudi in.

If you want money you'll have to produce something else. When you're selling knowledge you can't ask more than the buyer is likely to make from it. Philosophy, for instance, as taught by Mr Colombe in Florence, nets the prince at least 10,000 scudi a year. I know your laws on falling bodies have made a stir. They've applauded you in Prague and Paris. But the people who applaud don't pay Padua University what you cost it. You made an unfortunate choice of subject, Mr Galilei.

GALILEO: I see. Freedom of trade, freedom of research. Free trading in research, is that it?

PROCURATOR: Really, Mr Galilei, what a way of looking at it! Allow me to tell you that I don't quite understand your flippant remarks. Our Republic's thriving foreign trade hardly strikes me as a matter to be sneered at. And speaking from many years of experience as procurator of this university I would be even more disinclined to speak of scientific research in what I would term with respect, so frivolous a manner. *While Galileo glances longingly at his work table*: Consider the conditions that surround us. The slavery under whose whips the sciences in certain places are groaning. Whips cut from old leather bindings. Nobody there needs to know how a stone falls, merely what Aristotle wrote about it. Eyes are only for reading with. Why investigate falling bodies, when it's the laws governing grovelling bodies that count? Contrast the infinite joy with which our Republic welcomes your ideas, however daring they may be. Here you have a chance to research, to work. Nobody supervises you, nobody suppresses you. Our merchants know the value of better linen in their struggle with their competitors in Florence; they listen with interest to your cry for better physics, and physics in turn owes much to their cry for better looms. Our most prominent citizens take an interest in your researches, call on you, get you to demonstrate your findings: men whose time is precious. Don't underrate trade, Mr Galilei. Nobody here would stand for the slightest interference with your work or let outsiders make difficulties for you. This is a place where you can work, Mr Galilei, you have to admit it.

GALILEO *in despair*: Yes.

PROCURATOR: As for the material aspects: why can't you give us another nice piece of work like those famous proportional compasses of yours, the ones that allow complete mathematical dunces to trace lines, reckon compound interest on capital, reproduce a land survey on varying scales and determine the weight of cannon balls?

GALILEO: Kids' stuff.

PROCURATOR: Here's something that fascinated and astonished our top people and brought in good money, and you call it kids' stuff. I'm told even General Stefano Gritti can work out square roots with your instrument.

GALILEO: A real miracle. – All the same, Priuli, you've given me something to think about. Priuli, I think I might be able to let you have something of the kind you want. *He picks up the paper with the sketch.*

PROCURATOR: Could you? That would be the answer. *Gets up*: Mr Galilei, we realise that you are a great man. A great but dissatisfied man, if I may say so.

GALILEO: Yes, I am dissatisfied, and that's what you'd be paying me for if you had any brains. Because I'm dissatisfied with myself. But instead of doing that you force me to be dissatisfied with you. I admit I enjoy doing my stuff for you gentlemen of Venice in your famous arsenal and in the shipyards and cannon foundries. But you never give me the time to follow up the hunches which come to me there and which are important for my branch of science. That way you muzzle the threshing ox. I am 46 years old and have achieved nothing that satisfies me.

PROCURATOR: I mustn't interrupt you any longer.

GALILEO: Thank you.

Exit the Procurator.
Galileo is left alone for a moment or two and begins to work. Then
Andrea hurries in.

GALILEO *working*: Why didn't you eat the apple?

ANDREA: I need it to convince her that it turns.

GALILEO: Listen to me, Andrea: don't talk to other people about our ideas.

ANDREA: Why not?

GALILEO: The big shots won't allow it.

ANDREA: But it's the truth.

GALILEO: But they're forbidding it. – And there's something more. We physicists may think we have the answer, but that doesn't mean we can prove it. Even the ideas of a great man like Copernicus still need proving. They are only hypotheses. Give me those lenses.

ANDREA: Your half scudo wasn't enough. I had to leave my coat. As security.

GALILEO: How will you manage without a coat this winter?
Pause. Galileo arranges the lenses on the sheet with the sketch on it.

ANDREA: What's a hypothesis?

GALILEO: It's when you assume that something's likely, but haven't any facts. Look at Felicia down there outside the basket-maker's shop breastfeeding her child: it remains a hypothesis that she's giving it milk and not getting milk from it, till one actually goes and sees and proves it. Faced with the stars we are like dull-eyed worms that can hardly see at all. Those old constructions people have believed in for the last thousand years are hopelessly rickety: vast buildings most of whose wood is in the buttresses propping them up. Lots of laws that explain very little, whereas our new hypothesis has very few laws that explain a lot.

ANDREA: But you proved it all to me.

GALILEO: No, only that that's how it could be. I'm not saying it isn't a beautiful hypothesis; what's more there's nothing against it.

ANDREA: I'd like to be a physicist too, Mr Galilei.

GALILEO: That's understandable, given the million and one questions in our field still waiting to be cleared up. *He has gone to the window and looked through the lenses. Mildly interested*: Have a look through that, Andrea.

ANDREA: Holy Mary, it's all quite close. The bells in the campanile very close indeed. I can even read the copper letters: GRACIA DEI.

GALILEO: That'll get us 500 scudi.

2

Galileo presents the Venetian Republic with a new invention

No one's virtue is complete:
Great Galileo liked to eat.
You will not resent, we hope
The truth about his telescope.

The great arsenal of Venice, alongside the harbour.

Senators, headed by the Doge. To one side, Galileo's friend Sagredo and the fifteen-year-old Virginia Galilei with a velvet cushion on which rests a two-foot-long telescope in a crimson leather case. On a dais, Galileo. Behind him the telescope's stand, supervised by Feder-zoni the lens-grinder.

GALILEO: Your Excellency; august Signoria! In my capacity as mathematics teacher at your university in Padua and director of your great arsenal here in Venice I have always seen it as my job not merely to fulfil my exalted task as a teacher but also to provide useful inventions that would be of exceptional advantage to the Venetian Republic. Today it is with deep joy and all due deference that I find myself able to demonstrate and hand over to you a completely new instrument, namely my spyglass or telescope, fabricated in your world-famous Great Arsenal on the loftiest Christian and scientific principles, the product of seventeen years of patient research by your humble servant. *Galileo leaves the dais and stands alongside Sagredo. Applause. Galileo bows.*

GALILEO *softly to Sagredo*: Waste of time.

SAGREDO *softly*: You'll be able to pay the butcher, old boy.

GALILEO: Yes, they'll make money on this. *He bows again.*

PROCURATOR *steps on to the dais*: Your Excellency, august Signoria! Once again a glorious page in the great book of the arts is inscribed in a Venetian hand. *Polite applause*: Today a world-famous scholar is offering you, and you alone, a highly marketable tube, for you to manufacture and sell as and how you wish. *Louder applause*. What is more, has it struck you that in wartime this instrument will allow us to distinguish the number and types of the enemy's ships at least two hours before he does ours, with the result that we shall know how strong he is and be able to choose whether to pursue, join battle or run away? *Very loud applause*. And now, your Excellency, august Signoria, Mr Galileo invites you to accept this instrument which he has invented, this testimonial to his intuition, at the hand of his enchanting daughter.

Music. Virginia steps forward, bows and hands the telescope to the Procurator, who passes it to Federzoni. Federzoni puts it on the stand and focusses it. Doge and Senators mount the dais and look through the tube.

GALILEO *softly*: I'm not sure how long I'll be able to stick this circus. These people think they're getting a lucrative plaything, but it's a lot more than that. Last night I turned it on the moon.

SAGREDO: What did you see?

GALILEO: The moon doesn't generate its own light.

SAGREDO: What?

SENATORS: I can make out the fortifications of Santa Rosita, Mr Galilei. – They're having their dinner on that boat. Fried fish. Makes me feel peckish.

GALILEO: I'm telling you astronomy has stagnated for the last thousand years because they had no telescope.

SENATOR: Mr Galilei!

SAGREDO: They want you.

SENATOR: That contraption lets you see too much. I'll have to tell my women they can't take baths on the roof any longer.

GALILEO: Know what the Milky Way consists of?

SAGREDO: No.

GALILEO: I do.

SENATOR: One should be able to ask 10 scudi for a thing like that, Mr Galilei. *Galileo bows.*

VIRGINIA *leading Ludovico up to her father*: Ludovico wants to congratulate you, Father.

LUDOVICO *embarrassed*: I congratulate you, sir.

GALILEO: I've improved it.

LUDOVICO: Yes, sir. I see you've made the casing red. In Holland it was green.

GALILEO *turning to Sagredo*: I've even begun to wonder if I couldn't use it to prove a certain theory.

SAGREDO: Watch your step.

PROCURATOR: Your 500 scudi are in the bag, Galileo.

GALILEO *disregarding him*: Of course I'm sceptical about jumping to conclusions.

The Doge, a fat unassuming man, has come up to Galileo and is trying to address him with a kind of dignified awkwardness.

PROCURATOR: Mr Galilei, His Excellency the Doge.

The Doge shakes Galileo's hand.

GALILEO: Of course, the 500! Are you satisfied, your Excellency?

DOGE: I'm afraid our republic always has to have some pretext before the city fathers can do anything for our scholars.

PROCURATOR: But what other incentive can there be, Mr Galilei?

DOGE *smiling*: We need that pretext.

The Doge and the Procurator lead Galileo towards the Senators, who gather round him. Virginia and Ludovico slowly go away.

VIRGINIA: Did I do all right?

LUDOVICO: Seemed all right to me.

VIRGINIA: What's the matter?

LUDOVICO: Nothing, really. I suppose a green casing would have been just as good.

VIRGINIA: It strikes me they're all very pleased with Father.

LUDOVICO: And it strikes me I'm starting to learn a thing or two about science.

3

10 January 1610. Using the telescope, Galileo discovers celestial phenomena that confirm the Copernican system. Warned by his friend of the possible consequences of his research, Galileo proclaims his belief in human reason

> January ten, sixteen ten:
> Galileo Galilei abolishes heaven.

Galileo's study in Padua. Night. Galileo and Sagredo at the telescope, wrapped in heavy overcoats.

SAGREDO *looking through the telescope, half to himself*: The crescent's edge is quite irregular, jagged and rough. In the dark area, close to the luminous edge, there are bright spots.

They come up one after the other. The light starts from the spots and flows outwards over bigger and bigger surfaces, where it merges into the larger luminous part.

GALILEO: What's your explanation of these bright spots?

SAGREDO: It's not possible.

GALILEO: It is. They're mountains.

SAGREDO: On a star?

GALILEO: Huge mountains. Whose peaks are gilded by the rising sun while the surrounding slopes are still covered by night. What you're seeing is the light spreading down into the valleys from the topmost peaks.

SAGREDO: But this goes against two thousand years of astronomy.

GALILEO: It does. What you are seeing has been seen by no mortal except myself. You are the second.

SAGREDO: But the moon can't be an earth complete with mountains and valleys, any more than the earth can be a star.

GALILEO: The moon can be an earth complete with mountains and valleys, and the earth can be a star. An ordinary celestial body, one of thousands. Take another look. Does the dark part of the moon look completely dark to you?

SAGREDO: No. Now that I look at it, I can see a feeble ashy-grey light all over it.

GALILEO: What sort of light might that be?

SAGREDO: ?

GALILEO: It comes from the earth.

SAGREDO: You're talking through your hat. How can the earth give off light, with all its mountains and forests and waters; it's a cold body.

GALILEO: The same way the moon gives off light. Both of them are lit by the sun, and so they give off light. What the moon is to us, we are to the moon. It sees us sometimes as a crescent, sometimes as a half-moon, sometimes full and sometimes not at all.

SAGREDO: In other words, there's no difference between the moon and earth.

GALILEO: Apparently not.

SAGREDO: Ten years ago in Rome they burnt a man at the stake for that. His name was Giordano Bruno, and that is what he said.

GALILEO: Exactly. And that's what we can see. Keep your eye glued to the telescope, Sagredo, my friend. What you're seeing is the fact that there is no difference between heaven and earth. Today is 10 January 1610. Today mankind can write in its diary: Got rid of Heaven.

SAGREDO: That's frightful.

GALILEO: There is another thing I discovered. Perhaps it's more appalling still.

MRS SARTI *quietly*: Mr Procurator.

The Procurator rushes in.

PROCURATOR: I'm sorry to come so late. Do you mind if I speak to you alone?

GALILEO: Mr Sagredo can listen to anything I can, Mr Priuli.

PROCURATOR: But you may not exactly be pleased if the gentleman hears what has happened. Unhappily it is something quite unbelievable.

GALILEO: Mr Sagredo is quite used to encountering unbelievable when I am around, let me tell you.

PROCURATOR: No doubt, no doubt. *Pointing at the telescope*: Yes, that's the famous contraption. You might just as well throw it away. It's useless, utterly useless.

SAGREDO, *who has been walking around impatiently*: Why's that?

PROCURATOR: Are you aware that this invention of yours which you said was the fruit of seventeen years of research can be bought on any street corner in Italy for a few scudi? Made in Holland, what's more. There is a Dutch merchant-man unloading 500 telescopes down at the harbour at this very moment.

GALILEO: Really?

PROCURATOR: I find your equanimity hard to understand, sir.

SAGREDO: What are you worrying about? Thanks to this instrument, let me tell you, Mr Galilei has just made some revolutionary discoveries about the universe.

GALILEO *laughing*: Have a look, Priuli.

PROCURATOR: And let me tell you it's quite enough for me to have made my particular discovery, after getting Galileo's salary doubled for that piece of rubbish. It's a pure stroke of luck that the gentlemen of the signoria, in their confidence that they had secured the republic a monopoly of this instrument, didn't look through it and instantly see an ordinary streetseller at the nearest corner, magnified to the power of seven and hawking an identical tube for twice nothing. *Galileo laughs resoundingly.*

SAGREDO: My dear Mr Priuli. I may not be competent to judge this instrument's value for commerce but its value for philosophy is so boundless that . . .

PROCURATOR: For philosophy indeed. What's a mathematician like Mr Galilei got to do with philosophy? Mr Galilei, you did once invent a very decent water pump for the city and your irrigation system works well. The weavers too report favourably on your machine. So how was I to expect something like this?

GALILEO: Not so fast, Priuli. Sea passages are still long, hazardous and expensive. We need a clock in the sky we can rely on. A guide for navigation, right? Well, I have reason to believe that the telescope will allow us to make clear sightings of certain stars that execute extremely regular movements. New star charts might save our shipping several million scudi, Priuli.

PROCURATOR: Don't bother. I've listened too long already. In return for my help you've made me the laughing-stock of the city. I'll go down to history as the procurator who fell for a worthless telescope. It's all very well for you to laugh. You've got your 500 scudi. But I'm an honourable man, and I tell you this world turns my stomach.

He leaves, slamming the door.

GALILEO: He's really quite likeable when he's angry. Did you hear that? A world where one can't do business turns his stomach.

SAGREDO: Did you know about these Dutch instruments?

GALILEO: Of course, by hearsay. But the one I made these skinflints in the Signoria was twice as good. How am I supposed to work with the bailiffs in the house? And Virginia will soon have to have a dowry: she's not bright. Then I like buying books about other things besides physics, and I like a decent meal. Good meals are when I get most of my ideas. A degraded age! They were paying me less than the carter who drives their wine barrels. Four cords of firewood for two courses on mathematics. Now I've managed to squeeze 500 scudi out of them, but I've still got debts, including some dating from twenty years back. Give me five years off to research, and I'd have proved it all. I'm going to show you another thing.

SAGREDO *is reluctant to go to the telescope*: I feel something not all that remote from fear, Galileo.

GALILEO: I'm about to show you one of the shining milk-white clouds in the Milky Way. Tell me what it's made up of.

SAGREDO: They're stars, an infinite number.

GALILEO: In Orion alone there are 500 fixed stars. Those are the countless other worlds, the remote stars the man they burned talked about. He never saw them, he just expected them to be there.

SAGREDO: But even supposing our earth is a star, that's still a long way from Copernicus's view that it goes round the sun. There's not a star in the sky that has another star going round it. But the moon does go round the earth.

GALILEO: Sagredo, I wonder. I've been wondering since

the day before yesterday. Here we have Jupiter. *He focusses on it.* Round it we have four smaller neighbouring stars that are invisible except through the tube. I saw them on Monday but without bothering to note their position. Yesterday I looked again. I could swear the position of all four had changed. I noted them down. They've changed again. What's this? I saw four. *Agitated*: Have a look.

SAGREDO: I can see three.

GALILEO: Where's the fourth? There are the tables. We must work out what movements they might have performed. *Excited, they sit down to work. The stage darkens, but Jupiter and its accompanying stars can be seen on the cyclorama. As it grows light once more they are still sitting there in their winter coats.*

GALILEO: That's the proof. The fourth one can only have gone behind Jupiter, where it can't be seen. So here you've a star with another one going round it.

SAGREDO: What about the crystal sphere Jupiter is attached to?

GALILEO: Yes, where has it got to? How can Jupiter be attached if other stars circle round it? It's not some kind of prop in the sky, some base in the universe. It's another sun.

SAGREDO: Calm down. You're thinking too quickly.

GALILEO: What d'you mean, quickly? Wake up, man! You're seeing something nobody has ever seen before. They were right.

SAGREDO: Who, Copernicus and his lot?

GALILEO: And the other fellow. The whole world was against them, and they were right. Andrea must see this! *In great excitement he hurries to the door and shouts*: Mrs Sarti! Mrs Sarti!

SAGREDO: Don't get worked up, Galileo!

GALILEO: Get worked up, Sagredo! Mrs Sarti!

SAGREDO *turns the telescope away*: Stop bellowing like an idiot.

GALILEO: Stop standing there like a stuffed dummy when the truth has been found.

SAGREDO: I'm not standing like a stuffed dummy; I'm trembling with fear that it may be the truth.

GALILEO: Uh?

SAGREDO: Have you completely lost your head? Don't you realise what you'll be getting into if what you see there is true? And if you go round telling all and sundry that the earth is a planet and not the centre of the universe?

GALILEO: Right, and that the entire universe full of stars isn't turning around our tiny little earth, anyone could guess.

SAGREDO: In other words that it's just a lot of stars. Then where's God?

GALILEO: What d'you mean?

SAGREDO: God! Where is God?

GALILEO *angrily*: Not there anyway. Any more than he'd be here on earth, suppose there were creatures out there wanting to come and look for him.

SAGREDO: So where is God?

GALILEO: I'm not a theologian. I'm a mathematician.

SAGREDO: First and foremost you're a human being. And I'm asking: where is God in your cosmography?

GALILEO: Within ourselves or nowhere.

SAGREDO *shouting*: Like the man they burned said?

GALILEO: Like the man they burned said.

SAGREDO: That's what they burned him for. Less than ten years back.

GALILEO: Because he couldn't prove it. Because it was just a hypothesis. Mrs Sarti!

SAGREDO: Galileo, ever since I've known you you've known how to cover yourself. For seventeen years here in Padua and three more in Pisa you have been patiently teaching the Ptolemaic system proclaimed by the Church and confirmed by the writings the Church is based on. Like Copernicus you thought it was wrong but you taught it just the same.

GALILEO: Because I couldn't prove anything.

SAGREDO *incredulously*: And do you imagine that makes any difference!

GALILEO: A tremendous difference. Look, Sagredo, I believe in Humanity, which means to say I believe in human reason. If it weren't for that belief each morning I wouldn't have the power to get out of bed.

SAGREDO: Then let me tell you something. I don't. Forty years spent among human beings has again and again brought it home to me that they are not open to reason. Show them a comet with a red tail, scare them out of their wits, and they'll rush out of their houses and break their legs. But try making one rational statement to them, and back it up with seven proofs, and they'll just laugh at you.

GALILEO: That's quite untrue, and it's a slander. I don't see how you can love science if that's what you believe. Nobody who isn't dead can fail to be convinced by proof.

SAGREDO: How can you imagine their pathetic shrewdness has anything to do with reason?

GALILEO: I'm not talking about their shrewdness. I know they call a donkey a horse when they want to sell it and a horse a donkey when they want to buy. That's the kind of shrewdness you mean. But the horny-handed old woman who gives her mule an extra bundle of hay on the eve of a journey, the sea captain who allows for storms and doldrums when laying in stores, the child who puts on his cap once they have convinced him that it may rain: these are the people I pin my hopes to, because they all accept proof. Yes, I believe in reason's gentle tyranny over people. Sooner or later they have to give in to it. Nobody can go on indefinitely watching me – *he drops a pebble on the ground* – drop a pebble, then say it doesn't fall. No human being is capable of that. The lure of a proof is too great. Nearly everyone succumbs to it; sooner or later we all do. Thinking is one of the chief pleasures of the human race.

MRS SARTI *enters*: Do you want something, Mr Galilei?

GALILEO *who is back at his telescope making notes; in a very friendly voice*: Yes, I want Andrea.

MRS SARTI: Andrea? He's asleep in bed.

GALILEO: Can't you wake him up?

MRS SARTI: Why d'you want him?

GALILEO: I want to show him something he'll appreciate. He's to see something nobody but us two has seen since the earth was made.

MRS SARTI: Something more through your tube?

GALILEO: Something through my tube, Mrs Sarti.

MRS SARTI: And I'm to wake him up in the middle of the night for that? Are you out of your mind? He's got to have his sleep. I wouldn't think of waking him.

GALILEO: Definitely not?

MRS SARTI: Definitely not.

GALILEO: In that case, Mrs Sarti, perhaps you can help me. You see, a question has arisen where we can't agree, probably because both of us have read too many books. It's a question about the heavens, something to do with the stars. This is it: are we to take it that the greater goes round the smaller, or does the smaller go round the greater?

MRS SARTI *cautiously*: I never know where I am with you. Mr Galilei. Is that a serious question, or are you pulling my leg again?

GALILEO: A serious question.

MRS SARTI: Then I'll give you a quick answer. Do I serve your dinner or do you serve mine?

GALILEO: You serve mine. Yesterday it was burnt.

MRS SARTI: And why was it burnt? Because I had to fetch you your shoes in the middle of my cooking. Didn't I fetch you your shoes?

GALILEO: I suppose so.

MRS SARTI: You see, you're the one who has studied and is able to pay.

GALILEO: I see. I see there's no problem. Good night Mrs Sarti.

Mrs Sarti, amused, goes off.

GALILEO: Don't tell me people like that can't grasp the truth. They grab at it.

The bell has begun sounding for early morning Mass. Enter Virginia in a cloak, carrying a shielded light.

VIRGINIA: Good morning, Father.

GALILEO: Why are you up at this hour?

VIRGINIA: Mrs Sarti and I are going to early mass. Ludovico's coming too. What sort of night was it, Father?

GALILEO: Clear.

VIRGINIA: Can I have a look?

GALILEO: What for? *Virginia does not know what to say.* It's not a toy.

VIRGINIA: No, Father.

GALILEO: Anyhow the tube is a flop, so everybody will soon be telling you. You can get it for 3 scudi all over the place and the Dutch invented it ages ago.

VIRGINIA: Hasn't it helped you see anything fresh in the sky?

GALILEO: Nothing in your line. Just a few dim little spots to the left of a large planet; I'll have to do something to draw attention to them. *Talking past his daughter to Sagredo:* I might christen them 'the Medicean Stars' after the Grand-Duke of Florence. *Again to Virginia:* You'll be interested to hear, Virginia, that we'll probably be moving to Florence. I've written to them to ask if the Grand Duke can use me as his court mathematician.

VIRGINIA *radiant:* At Court?

SAGREDO: Galileo!

GALILEO: My dear fellow, I'll need time off. I need proofs. And I want the fleshpots. And here's a job where I won't have to take private pupils and din the Ptolemaic system into them, but shall have the time, time, time, time, time –

to work out my proofs; because what I've got so far isn't enough. It's nothing, just wretched odds and ends. I can't take on the whole world with that. There's not a single shred of proof to show that any heavenly body whatever goes round the sun. But I am going to produce the proofs, proofs for everyone, from Mrs Sarti right up to the Pope. The only thing that worries me is whether the court will have me.

VIRGINIA: Of course they'll have you, Father, with your new stars and all that.

GALILEO: Run along to your mass.

Exit Virginia.

GALILEO: I'm not used to writing to important people. *He hands Sagredo a letter.* Do you think this is well expressed?

SAGREDO *reads out the end of the letter*: 'My most ardent desire is to be closer to you, the rising sun that will illuminate this age.' The grand duke of Florence is aged nine.

GALILEO: That's it. I see; you think my letter is too submissive. I'm wondering if it is submissive enough – not too formal, lacking in authentic servility. A reticent letter would be all right for someone whose distinction it is to have proved Aristotle correct, but not for me. A man like me can only get a halfway decent job by crawling on his belly. And you know what I think of people whose brains aren't capable of filling their stomachs.

Mrs Sarti and Virginia pass the men on their way to mass.

SAGREDO: Don't go to Florence, Galileo.

GALILEO: Why not?

SAGREDO: Because it's run by monks.

GALILEO: The Florentine Court includes eminent scholars.

SAGREDO: Flunkeys.

GALILEO: I'll take them by the scruff of the neck and I'll drag them to the telescope. Even monks are human beings, Sagredo. Even they are subject to the seduction of proof. Copernicus, don't forget, wanted them to believe his figures;

but I only want them to believe their eyes. If the truth is too feeble to stick up for itself then it must go over to the attack. I'm going to take them by the scruff of the neck and force them to look through this telescope.

SAGREDO: Galileo, I see you embarking on a frightful road. It is a disastrous night when mankind sees the truth. And a delusive hour when it believes in human reason. What kind of person is said to go into things with his eyes open? One who is going to his doom. How could the people in power give free rein to somebody who knows the truth, even if it concerns the remotest stars? Do you imagine the Pope will hear the truth when you tell him he's wrong, and not just hear that he's wrong? Do you imagine he will merely note in his diary: January 10th 1610 – got rid of heaven? How can you propose to leave the Republic with the truth in your pocket, risking the traps set by monks and princes and brandishing your tube. You may be a sceptic in science, but you're childishly credulous as soon as anything seems likely to help you to pursue it. You don't believe in Aristotle, but you do believe in the Grand Duke of Florence. Just now, when I was watching you at the telescope and you were watching those new stars, it seemed to me I was watching you stand on blazing faggots; and when you said you believed in proof I smelt burnt flesh. I am fond of science, my friend, but I am fonder of you. Don't go to Florence, Galileo.

GALILEO: If they'll have me I shall go.

On a curtain appears the last page of his letter:

In giving the noble name of the house of Medici to the new stars which I have discovered I realise that whereas the old gods and heroes were immortalised by being raised to the realm of the stars in this case the noble name of Medici will ensure that these stars are remembered for ever. For my own part I commend myself to you as one of your loyalest and most humble servants who considers it the height of privilege to have been born as your subject.

There is nothing for which I long more ardently than to be closer to you, the rising sun which will illuminate this epoch.

Galileo Galilei.

4

Galileo has exchanged the Venetian Republic for the Court of Florence. His discoveries with the telescope are not believed by the court scholars

The old says: What I've always done I'll always do.
The new says: If you're useless you must go.

Galileo's house in Florence. Mrs Sarti is preparing Galileo's study for the reception of guests. Her son Andrea is sitting tidying the star charts.

MRS SARTI: There has been nothing but bowing and scraping ever since we arrived safe and sound in this marvellous Florence. The whole city files past the tube, with me mopping the floor after them. If there was anything to all these discoveries the clergy would be the first to know. I spent four years in service with Monsignor Filippo without every managing to get all his library dusted. Leather bound books up to the ceiling – and no slim volumes of poetry either. And that good Monsignor had a whole cluster of sores on his bottom from sitting and poring over all that learning; d'you imagine a man like that doesn't know the answers? And today's grand visit will be such a disaster that I'll never be able to meet the milkman's eye tomorrow. I knew what I was about when I advised him to give the gentlemen a good supper first, a proper joint of lamb, before they inspect his tube. But no: *she imitates Galileo*: 'I've got something else for them.'

There is knocking downstairs.

MRS SARTI *looks through the spyhole in the window*: My goodness, the Grand Duke's arrived. And Galileo is still at the University.

She hurries down the stairs and admits the Grand Duke of Tuscany, Cosimo de Medici, together with his chamberlain and two court ladies.

COSIMO: I want to see that tube.

CHAMBERLAIN: Perhaps your Highness will possess himself until Mr Galilei and the other university gentlemen have arrived. *To Mrs Sarti*: Mr Galileo was going to ask our astronomers to test his newly discovered so-called Medicean stars.

COSIMO: They don't believe in the tube, not for one moment. So where is it?

MRS SARTI: Upstairs in the study.

The boy nods, points up the staircase and runs up it at a nod from Mrs Sarti.

CHAMBERLAIN *a very old man*: Your Highness! *To Mrs Sarti*: Have we *got* to go up there? I wouldn't have come at all if his tutor had not been indisposed.

MRS SARTI: The young gentleman will be all right. My own boy is up there.

COSIMO *entering above*: Good evening!

The two boys bow ceremoniously to each other. Pause. Then Andrea turns back to his work.

ANDREA *very like his master*: This place is getting like a pigeon loft.

COSIMO: Plenty of visitors?

ANDREA: Stump around here staring, and don't know the first thing.

COSIMO: I get it. That the . . .? *Pointing to the telescope.*

ANDREA: Yes, that's it. Hands off, though.

COSIMO: And what's that? *He points to the wooden model of the Ptolemaic system.*

ANDREA: That's Ptolemy's thing.

COSIMO: Showing how the sun goes round, is that it?

ANDREA: So they say.

COSIMO *sitting down on a chair, takes the model on his lap*: My tutor's got a cold. I got off early. It's all right here.

ANDREA *shambles around restlessly and irresolutely shooting doubtful looks at the unknown boy, then finds that he cannot hold out any longer, and brings out a second model from behind the maps, one representing the Copernican system*: But really it's like this.

COSIMO: What's like this?

ANDREA *pointing at Cosimo's model*: That's how people think it is and – *pointing at his own* – this is how it is really. The earth turns round the sun, get it?

COSIMO: D'you really mean that?

ANDREA: Sure, it's been proved.

COSIMO: Indeed? I'd like to know why I'm never allowed to see the old man now. Yesterday he came to supper again.

ANDREA: They don't believe it, do they?

COSIMO: Of course they do.

ANDREA *suddenly pointing at the model on Cosimo's lap*: Give it back: you can't even understand that one.

COSIMO: Why should you have two?

ANDREA: Just you hand it over. It's not a toy for kids.

COSIMO: No reason why I shouldn't give it to you, but you need to learn some manners, you know.

ANDREA: You're an idiot, and to hell with manners, just give it over or you'll start something.

COSIMO: Hands off, I tell you.

They start brawling and are soon tangled up on the floor.

ANDREA: I'll teach you to handle a model properly! Say 'pax'.

COSIMO: It's broken. You're twisting my hand.

ANDREA: We'll see who's right. Say it turns or I'll bash you.

COSIMO: Shan't. Stop it, Ginger. I'll teach you manners.

ANDREA: Ginger: who are you calling Ginger?

They go on brawling in silence. Enter Galileo and a group of university professors downstairs. Federzoni follows.

CHAMBERLAIN: Gentlemen, his highness's tutor Mr Suri has a slight indisposition and was therefore unable to accompany his highness.

THEOLOGIAN: I hope it's nothing serious.

CHAMBERLAIN: Not in the least.

GALILEO *disappointed*: Isn't his highness here?

CHAMBERLAIN: His highness is upstairs. Please don't let me detain you. The court is so very eager to know what our distinguished university thinks about Mr Galileo's remarkable instrument and these amazing new stars.

They go upstairs.

The boys are now lying quiet, having heard the noise downstairs.

COSIMO: Here they are. Let me get up.

They stand up quickly.

THE GENTLEMEN *on their way upstairs*: No, there's nothing whatever to worry about. – Those cases in the old city: our faculty of medicine says there's no question of it being plague. Any miasmas would freeze at this temperature. – The worst possible thing in such a situation is to panic. – It's just the usual incidence of colds for this time of year. – Every suspicion has been eliminated. – Nothing whatever to worry about.

Greetings upstairs.

GALILEO: Your highness, I am glad to be able to introduce the gentlemen of your university to these new discoveries in your presence.

Cosimo bows formally in all directions, including Andrea's.

THEOLOGIAN *noticing the broken Ptolemaic model on the floor*: Something seems to have got broken here.

Cosimo quickly stoops down and politely hands Andrea the model. Meantime Galileo unobtrusively shifts the other model to one side.

GALILEO *at the telescope*: As your highness no doubt realises, we astronomers have been running into great difficulties in our calculations for some while. We have been using a very ancient system which is apparently consistent with our philosophy but not, alas, with the facts. Under this ancient, Ptolemaic system the motions of the stars are presumed to be extremely complex. The planet Venus, for instance, is supposed to have an orbit like this. *On a board he draws the epicyclical orbit of Venus according to the Ptolemaic hypothesis.* But even if we accept the awkwardness of such motions we are still unable to predict the position of the stars accurately. We do not find them where in principle they ought to be. What is more, some stars perform motions which the Ptolemaic system just cannot explain. Such motions, it seems to me, are performed by certain small stars which I have recently discovered around the planet Jupiter. Would you gentlemen care to start by observing these satellites of Jupiter, the Medicean stars?

ANDREA *indicating the stool by the telescope*: Kindly sit here.

PHILOSOPHER: Thank you, my boy. I fear things are not quite so simple. Mr Galileo, before turning to your famous tube, I wonder if we might have the pleasure of a disputation? Its subject to be: Can such planets exist?

MATHEMATICIAN: A formal dispute.

GALILEO: I was thinking you could just look through the telescope and convince yourselves?

ANDREA: This way, please.

MATHEMATICIAN: Of course, of course. I take it you are familiar with the opinion of the ancients that there can be no stars which turn round centres other than the earth, nor any which lack support in the sky?

GALILEO: I am.

PHILOSOPHER: Moreover, quite apart from the very possibility of such stars, which our mathematician – *he turns towards the mathematician* – would appear to doubt, I would like in all humility to pose the philosophical question: are such stars necessary? Aristotelis divini universum . . .

GALILEO: Shouldn't we go on using the vernacular? My colleague Mr Federzoni doesn't understand Latin.

PHILOSOPHER: Does it matter if he understands us or not?

GALILEO: Yes.

PHILOSOPHER: I am so sorry. I thought he was your lens-grinder.

ANDREA: Mr Federzoni is a lens-grinder and a scholar.

PHILOSOPHER: Thank you, my boy. Well, if Mr Federzoni insists . . .

GALILEO: I insist.

PHILOSOPHER: The argument will be less brilliant, but it's your house. The universe of the divine Aristotle, with the mystical music of its spheres and its crystal vaults, the orbits of its heavenly bodies, the slanting angle of the sun's course, the secrets of the moon tables, the starry richness catalogued in the southern hemisphere and the transparent structure of the celestial globe add up to an edifice of such exquisite proportions that we should think twice before disrupting its harmony.

GALILEO: How about your highness now taking a look at his impossible and unnecessary stars through this telescope?

MATHEMATICIAN: One might be tempted to answer that, if your tube shows something which cannot be there, it cannot be an entirely reliable tube, wouldn't you say?

GALILEO: What d'you mean by that?

MATHEMATICIAN: It would be rather more appropriate, Mr Galileo, if you were to name your reasons for assuming that there could be free-floating stars moving about in the highest sphere of the unalterable heavens.

PHILOSOPHER: Your reasons, Mr Galileo, your reasons.

GALILEO: My reasons! When a single glance at the stars

themselves and my own notes makes the phenomenon evident? Sir, your disputation is becoming absurd.

MATHEMATICIAN: If one could be sure of not over-exciting you one might say that what is in your tube and what is in the skies is not necessarily the same thing.

PHILOSOPHER: That couldn't be more courteously put.

FEDERZONI: They think we painted the Medicean stars on the lens.

GALILEO: Are you saying I'm a fraud?

PHILOSOPHER: How could we? In his highness's presence too.

MATHEMATICIAN: Your instrument – I don't know whether to call it your brainchild or your adopted brainchild – is most ingeniously made, no doubt of that.

PHILOSOPHER: And we are utterly convinced, Mr Galilei, that neither you nor anyone else would bestow the illustrious name of our ruling family on stars whose existence was not above all doubt. *All bow deeply to the grand duke.*

COSIMO *turns to the ladies of the court*: Is something the matter with my stars?

THE OLDER COURT LADY: There is nothing the matter with your highness's stars. It's just that the gentlemen are wondering if they are really and truly there.
Pause.

THE YOUNGER COURT LADY: I'm told you can actually see the wheels on the Plough.

FEDERZONI: Yes, and all kinds of things on the Bull.

GALILEO: Well, are you gentlemen going to look through it or not?

PHILOSOPHER: Of course, of course.

MATHEMATICIAN: Of course.
Pause. Suddenly Andrea turns and walks stiffly out across the whole length of the room. His mother stops him.

MRS SARTI: What's the matter with you?

ANDREA: They're stupid. *He tears himself away and runs off.*

PHILOSOPHER: A lamentable boy.

CHAMBERLAIN: Your highness: gentlemen: may I remind you that the state ball is due to start in three quarters of an hour.

MATHEMATICIAN: Let's not beat about the bush. Sooner or later Mr Galilei will have to reconcile himself to the facts. Those Jupiter satellites of his would penetrate the crystal spheres. It is as simple as that.

FEDERZONI: You'll be surprised: the crystal spheres don't exist.

PHILOSOPHER: Any textbook will tell you that they do, my good man.

FEDERZONI: Right, then let's have new textbooks.

PHILOSOPHER: Your highness, my distinguished colleague and I are supported by none less than the divine Aristotle himself.

GALILEO *almost obsequiously*: Gentlemen, to believe in the authority of Aristotle is one thing, tangible facts are another. You are saying that according to Aristotle there are crystal spheres up there, so certain motions just cannot take place because the stars would penetrate them. But suppose those motions could be established? Mightn't that suggest to you that those crystal spheres don't exist? Gentlemen, in all humility I ask you to go by the evidence of your eyes.

MATHEMATICIAN: My dear Galileo, I may strike you as very old-fashioned, but I'm in the habit of reading Aristotle now and again, and there, I can assure you, I trust the evidence of my eyes.

GALILEO: I am used to seeing the gentlemen of the various faculties shutting their eyes to every fact and pretending that nothing has happened. I produce my observations and everyone laughs: I offer my telescope so they can see for themselves, and everyone quotes Aristotle.

FEDERZONI: The fellow had no telescope.

MATHEMATICIAN: That's just it.

PHILOSOPHER *grandly*: If Aristotle is going to be dragged in the mud – that's to say an authority recognized not only by every classical scientist but also by the chief fathers of the church – then any prolonging of this discussion is in my view a waste of time. I have no use for discussions which are not objective. Basta.

GALILEO: Truth is born of the times, not of authority. Our ignorance is limitless: let us lop one cubic millimeter off it. Why try to be clever now that we at last have a chance of being just a little less stupid? I have had the unimaginable luck to get my hands on a new instrument that lets us observe one tiny corner of the universe a little, but not all that much, more exactly. Make use of it.

PHILOSOPHER: Your highness, ladies and gentlemen, I just wonder where all this is leading?

GALILEO: I should say our duty as scientists is not to ask where truth is leading.

PHILOSOPHER *agitatedly*: Mr Galilei, truth might lead us anywhere!

GALILEO: Your highness. At night nowadays telescopes are being pointed at the sky all over Italy. Jupiter's moons may not bring down the price of milk. But they have never been seen before, and yet all the same they exist. From this the man in the street concludes that a lot else might exist if only he opened his eyes. It is your duty to confirm this. What has made Italy prick up its ears is not the movements of a few distant stars but the news that hitherto unquestioned dogmas have begun to totter – and we all know that there are too many of those. Gentlemen, don't let us fight for questionable truths.

FEDERZONI: You people are teachers: you should be stimulating the questions.

PHILOSOPHER: I would rather your man didn't tell us how to conduct a scholarly disputation.

GALILEO: Your highness! My work in the Great Arsenal in Venice brought me into daily contact with draughtsmen, builders and instrument mechanics. Such people showed me a lot of new approaches. They don't read much, but rely on the evidence of their five senses, without all that much fear as to where such evidence is going to lead them . . .

PHILOSOPHER: Oho!

GALILEO: Very much like our mariners who a hundred years ago abandoned our coasts without knowing what other coasts they would encounter, if any. It looks as if the only way today to find that supreme curiosity which was the real glory of classical Greece is to go down to the docks.

PHILOSOPHER: After what we've heard so far I've no doubt that Mr Galilei will find admirers at the docks.

CHAMBERLAIN: Your highness, I am dismayed to note that this exceptionally instructive conversation has become a trifle prolonged. His highness must have some repose before the court ball.

At a sign, the grand duke bows to Galileo. The court quickly gets ready to leave.

MRS SARTI *blocks the grand duke's way and offers him a plate of biscuits*: A biscuit, your highness? *The Older court lady leads the grand duke out.*

GALILEO *hurrying after them*: But all you gentlemen need do is look through the telescope!

CHAMBERLAIN: His highness will not fail to submit your ideas to our greatest living astronomer: Father Christopher Clavius, chief astronomer at the papal college in Rome.

5

Undeterred even by the plague, Galileo carries on with his researches

(a)

Early morning. Galileo at the telescope, bent over his notes. Enter Virginia with a travelling bag.

GALILEO: Virginia! Has something happened?

VIRGINIA: The convent's shut; they sent us straight home. Arcetri has had five cases of plague.

GALILEO *calls*: Sarti!

VIRGINIA: Market Street was barricaded off last night. Two people have died in the old town, they say, and there are three more dying in hospital.

GALILEO: As usual they hushed it all up till it was too late.

MRS SARTI *entering*: What are you doing here?

VIRGINIA: The plague.

MRS SARTI: God alive! I'll pack. *Sits down.*

GALILEO: Pack nothing. Take Virginia and Andrea. I'll get my notes.

He hurries to his table and hurriedly gathers up papers. Mrs Sarti puts Andrea's coat on him as he runs up, then collects some food and bed linen. Enter a grand-ducal footman.

FOOTMAN: In view of the spread of the disease his highness has left the city for Bologna. However, he insisted that Mr Galilei too should be offered a chance to get to safety. The carriage will be outside your door in two minutes.

MRS SARTI *to Virginia and Andrea*: Go outside at once. Here, take this.

ANDREA: What for? If you don't tell me why I shan't go.

MRS SARTI: It's the plague, my boy.

VIRGINIA: We'll wait for Father.

MRS SARTI: Mr Galilei, are you ready?

GALILEO *wrapping the telescope in the tablecloth*: Put Virginia and Andrea in the carriage. I won't be a moment.

VIRGINIA: No, we're not going without you. Once you start packing up your books you'll never finish.

MRS SARTI: The coach is there.

GALILEO: Have some sense, Virginia, if you don't take your seats the coachman will drive off. Plague is no joking matter.

VIRGINIA *protesting, as Mrs Sarti and Andrea escort her out*: Help him with his books, or he won't come.

MRS SARTI *from the main door*: Mr Galilei, the coachman says he can't wait.

GALILEO: Mrs Sarti, I don't think I should go. It's all such a mess, you see: three months' worth of notes which I might as well throw away if I can't spend another night or two on them. Anyway this plague is all over the place.

MRS SARTI: Mr Galilei! You must come now! You're crazy.

GALILEO: You'll have to go off with Virginia and Andrea. I'll follow.

MRS SARTI: Another hour, and nobody will be able to get away. You must come. *Listens*. He's driving off. I'll have to stop him.
Exit.
Galileo walks up and down. Mrs Sarti re-enters, very pale. without her bundle.

GALILEO: What are you still here for? You'll miss the children's carriage.

MRS SARTI: They've gone. Virginia had to be held in. The children will get looked after in Bologna. But who's going to see you get your meals?

GALILEO: You're crazy. Staying in this city in order to cook!
Picking up his notes: Don't think I'm a complete fool, Mrs

Sarti. I can't abandon these observations. I have powerful enemies and I must collect proofs for certain hypotheses.

MRS SARTI: You don't have to justify yourself. But it's not exactly sensible.

(b)

Outside Galileo's house in Florence. Galileo steps out and looks down the street. Two nuns pass by.

GALILEO *addresses them*: Could you tell me, sisters, where I can buy some milk? The milk woman didn't come this morning, and my housekeeper has left.

ONE NUN: The only shops open are in the lower town.

THE OTHER NUN: Did you come from here? *Galileo nods.* This is the street!

The two nuns cross themselves, mumble a Hail Mary and hurry away. A man goes by.

GALILEO *addresses him*: Aren't you the baker that delivers our bread to us? *The man nods.* Have you seen my housekeeper? She must have left last night. She hasn't been around all day. *The man shakes his head. A window is opened across the way and a woman looks out.*

WOMAN *yelling*: Hurry! They've got the plague opposite! *The man runs off horrified.*

GALILEO: Have you heard anything about my housekeeper?

WOMAN: Your housekeeper collapsed in the street up there. She must have realised. That's why she went. So inconsiderate!

She slams the window shut.

Children come down the street. They see Galileo and run away screaming. Galileo turns round; two soldiers hurry up, encased in armour.

SOLDIERS: Get right back indoors!

They push Galileo back into his house with their long pikes. They bolt the door behind him.

GALILEO *at the window*: Can you tell me what happened to the woman?

SOLDIERS: They throw them on the heap.

WOMAN *reappears at the window*: That whole street back there is infected. Why can't you close it off?

The soldiers rope the street off.

WOMAN: But that way nobody can get into our house. This part doesn't have to be closed off. This part's all right. Stop it! Stop! Can't you listen? My husband's still in town, he won't be able to get through to us. You animals! *She can be heard inside weeping and screaming. The soldiers leave. At another window an old woman appears.*

GALILEO: That must be a fire back there.

THE OLD WOMAN: They've stopped putting them out where there's any risk of infection. All they can think about is the plague.

GALILEO: Just like them. It's their whole system of government. Chopping us off like the diseased branch of some barren figtree.

THE OLD WOMAN: That's not fair. It's just that they're powerless.

GALILEO: Are you the only one in your house?

THE OLD WOMAN: Yes. My son sent me a note. Thank God he got a message last night to say somebody back there had died, so he didn't come home. There were eleven cases in our district during the night.

GALILEO: I blame myself for not making my housekeeper leave in time. I had some urgent work, but she had no call to stay.

THE OLD WOMAN: We can't leave either. Who's to take us in? No need for you to blame yourself. I saw her. She left early this morning, around seven o'clock. She must have been ill; when she saw me coming out to fetch in the bread she deliberately kept away from me. She didn't want them to close off your house. But they're bound to find out.

A rattling sound is heard.

GALILEO: What's that?

THE OLD WOMAN: They're trying to make noises to drive away the clouds with the plague seeds in them.

Galileo roars with laughter.

THE OLD WOMAN: Fancy being able to laugh now.

A man comes down the street and finds it roped off.

GALILEO: Hey, you! This street's closed off and I've nothing to eat. Hey! Hey!

The man has quickly hurried away.

THE OLD WOMAN: They may bring something. If not I can leave a jug of milk outside your door tonight, if you're not scared.

GALILEO: Hey! Hey! Can't anybody hear us?

All of a sudden Andrea is standing by the rope. He has been crying.

GALILEO: Andrea! How did you get here?

ANDREA: I was here first thing. I knocked but you didn't open your door. They told me you . . .

GALILEO: Didn't you go off in the carriage?

ANDREA: Yes. But I managed to jump out. Virginia went on. Can't I come in?

THE OLD WOMAN: No, you can't. You'll have to go to the Ursulines. Your mother may be there.

ANDREA: I've been. But they wouldn't let me see her. She's too ill.

GALILEO: Did you walk the whole way back? It's three days since you left, you know.

ANDREA: It took all that time. Don't be cross with me. They arrested me once.

GALILEO *helplessly*: Don't cry. You know, I've found out lots of things since you went. Shall I tell you? *Andrea nods between his sobs.* Listen carefully or you won't understand. You remember me showing you the planet Venus? Don't bother about that noise, it's nothing. Can you remember? You know what I saw? It's like the moon! I've seen it as a half-circle and I've seen it as a sickle. What d'you say to that? I can demonstrate the whole thing to you with a lamp and a small ball. That proves it's yet another planet with no light of its own. And it turns round the sun in a simple circle; isn't that marvellous?

ANDREA *sobbing*: Yes, and that's a fact.

GALILEO *quietly*: I never asked her to stay.

Andrea says nothing

GALILEO: But of course if I hadn't stayed myself it wouldn't have happened.

ANDREA: They'll have to believe you now, won't they?

GALILEO: I've got all the proofs I need now. Once this is over, I tell you, I shall go to Rome and show them.

Down the street come two masked men with long poles and buckets. They use these to pass bread through the window to Galileo and the old woman.

THE OLD WOMAN: And there's a woman across there with three children. Leave something for her too.

GALILEO: But I've got nothing to drink. There's no water left in the house. *The two shrug their shoulders.* Will you be coming back tomorrow?

ONE MAN *in a muffled voice, since he has a rag over his mouth*: Who knows what'll happen tomorrow?

GALILEO: If you do come, could you bring me a small book I need for my work?

THE MAN *gives a stifled laugh*: As if a book could make any difference. You'll be lucky if you get bread.

GALILEO: But this boy is my pupil, and he'll be there and can give it you for me. It's the chart giving the periodicity of Mercury, Andrea: I've mislaid it. Can you get me one from the school?

The men have gone on.

ANDREA: Of course. I'll get it, Mr Galilei. *Exit. Galileo likewise goes in. The old woman comes out of the house opposite and puts a jug outside Galileo's door.*

6

1616. The Vatican research institute, the Collegium Romanum, confirms Galileo's findings

> Things take indeed a wondrous turn
> When learned men do stoop to learn.
> Clavius, we are pleased to say
> Upheld Galileo Galilei.

Hall of the Collegium Romanum in Rome. It is night-time. High ecclesiastics, monks and scholars in groups. On his own, to one side, Galileo. The atmosphere is extremely hilarious. Before the beginning of the scene a great wave of laughter is heard.

A FAT PRELATE *clasps his belly with laughing*: Stupidity! Stupidity! I'd like to hear a proposition that people won't believe.

A SCHOLAR: For instance: that you have an incurable aversion to meals, Monsignor.

A FAT PRELATE: They'd believe it; they'd believe it. Things have to make sense to be disbelieved. That Satan exists: that's something they doubt. But that the earth spins round like a marble in the gutter; that's believed all right. O sancta simplicatas!

A MONK *play-acting*: I'm getting giddy. The earth's spinning round too fast. Permit me to hold on to you, professor. *He pretends to lurch and clutches one of the scholars.*

THE SCHOLAR *following suit*: Yes, the old girl has been on the bottle again.

He clutches another.

THE MONK: Stop, stop! We're skidding off. Stop, I said!

A SECOND SCHOLAR: Venus is all askew. I can only see one half of her backside. Help!

A group of laughing monks forms, acting as if they were doing their best not to be swept off a ship's deck in a storm.

A SECOND MONK: As long as we aren't flung on to the moon! It's said to have terribly sharp peaks, my brethren.

THE FIRST SCHOLAR: Dig your heels in and resist.

THE FIRST MONK: And don't look down. I'm losing my balance.

THE FAT PRELATE *intentionally loudly, aiming at Galileo*: Oh, that's impossible. Nobody is unbalanced in the Collegium Romanum.

Much laughter. Two of the Collegium astronomers enter from a door. There is a silence.

A MONK: Are you still going over it? That's scandalous.

THE FIRST ASTRONOMER *angrily*: Not us.

THE SECOND ASTRONOMER: What's this meant to lead to? I don't understand Clavius's attitude ... One can't treat everything as gospel that has been put forward in the past fifty years. In 1572 a new star appeared in the eighth and highest sphere, the sphere of the fixed stars, which seemed larger and more brilliant than all the stars round it, and within eighteen months it had gone out and been annihilated. Does that mean we must question the eternity and immutability of the heavens?

PHILOSOPHER: Give them half a chance and they'll smash up our whole starry sky.

THE FIRST ASTRONOMER: Yes, what are we coming to? Five years later Tycho Brahe in Denmark established the course of a comet. It started above the moon and broke through one crystal sphere after another, the solid supports on which all the moving of the heavenly bodies depend. It encountered no obstacles, there was no deflection of its light. Does that mean we must doubt the existence of the spheres?

THE PHILOSOPHER: It's out of the question. As Italy's and

the Church's greatest astronomer, how can Christopher Clavius stoop to examine such a proposition?

THE FAT PRELATE: Outrageous.

THE FIRST ASTRONOMER: He is examining it, though. He's sitting in there staring through that diabolical tube.

THE SECOND ASTRONOMER: Principiis obsta! It all started when we began reckoning so many things – the length of the solar year, the dates of solar and lunar eclipses, the position of the heavenly bodies – according to the tables established by Copernicus, who was a heretic.

A MONK: Which is better, I ask you: to have an eclipse of the moon happen three days later than the calendar says, or never to have eternal salvation at all?

A VERY THIN MONK *comes forward with an open bible, fanatically thrusting his finger at a certain passage*: What do the Scriptures say? "Sun, stand thou still on Gibeon and thou, moon, in the valley of Ajalon." How can the sun stand still if it never moves at all as suggested by this heretic? Are the Scriptures lying?

THE FIRST ASTRONOMER: No, and that's why we walked out.

THE SECOND ASTRONOMER: There *are* phenomena that present difficulties for us astronomers, but does mankind have to understand everything? *Both go out.*

THE VERY THIN MONK: They degrade humanity's dwelling place to a wandering star. Men, animals, plants and the kingdoms of the earth get packed on a cart and driven in a circle round an empty sky. Heaven and earth are no longer distinct, according to them. Heaven because it is made of earth, and earth because it is just one more heavenly body. There is no more difference between top and bottom, between eternal and ephemeral. That we are short-lived we know. Now they tell us that heaven is short-lived too. There are sun, moon and stars, and we live on the earth, it used to be said, and so the Book has it; but now these people are saying the earth is another star. Wait till they say man and animal are not distinct either, man himself is an animal, there's nothing but animals!

THE FIRST SCHOLAR *to Galileo*: Mr Galilei, you've let something fall.

GALILEO *who had meanwhile taken his stone from his pocket, played with it and finally allowed it to drop on the floor, bending to pick it up*: Rise, monsignor; I let it rise.

THE FAT PRELATE *turning round*: An arrogant fellow.

Enter a very old cardinal supported by a monk. They respectfully make way for him.

THE VERY OLD CARDINAL: Are they still in there? Can't they settle such a trivial matter more quickly? Clavius must surely know his astronomy. I am told that this Mr Galilei moves mankind away from the centre of the universe and dumps it somewhere on the edge. Clearly this makes him an enemy of the human race. We must treat him as such. Mankind is the crown of creation, as every child knows, God's highest and dearest creature. How could He take something so miraculous, the fruit of so much effort, and lodge it on a remote, minor, constantly elusive star? Would he send His Son to such a place? How can there be people so perverse as to pin their faith to these slaves of the multiplication table! Which of God's creatures would stand for anything like that?

THE FAT PRELATE *murmurs*: The gentleman is present.

THE VERY OLD CARDINAL *to Galileo*: It's you, is it? You know, my eyesight is not what it was, but I can still see one thing: that you bear a remarkable likeness to what's-his-name, you know, that man we burned.

THE MONK: Your Eminence should avoid excitement. The doctor . . .

THE VERY OLD CARDINAL *shakes him off. To Galileo*: You want to debase the earth even though you live on it and derive everything from it. You are fouling your own nest.

But I for one am not going to stand for that. *He pushes the monk away and begins proudly striding to and fro.* I am not just any old creature on any insignificant star briefly circling in no particular place. I am walking, with a firm step, on a fixed earth, it is motionless, it is the centre of the universe, I am at the centre and the eye of the Creator falls upon me and me alone. Round about me, attached to eight crystal spheres, revolve the fixed stars and the mighty sun which has been created to light my surroundings. And myself too, that God may see me. In this way everything comes visibly and incontrovertibly to depend on me, mankind, God's great effort, the creature on whom it all centres, made in God's own image, indestructible and . . . *He collapses.*

THE MONK: Your Eminence has overstrained himself.

At this moment the door at the back opens and the great Clavius enters at the head of his astronomers. Swiftly and in silence he crosses the hall without looking to one side or the other and addresses a monk as he is on the way out.

CLAVIUS: He's right. *He leaves, followed by the astronomers. The door at the back remains open. Deadly silence. The very old Cardinal recovers consciousness.*

THE VERY OLD CARDINAL: What's that? Have they reached a conclusion?

Nobody dares tell him.

THE MONK: Your Eminence must be taken home. *The old man is assisted out. All leave the hall, worried. A little monk from Clavius's committee of experts pauses beside Galileo.*

THE LITTLE MONK *confidentially*: Mr Galilei, before he left Father Clavius said: Now it's up to the theologians to see how they can straighten out the movements of the heavens once more. You've won. *Exit*

GALILEO *tries to hold him back*: It has won. Not me: reason has won.

The little monk has already left. Galileo too starts to go. In the doorway he encounters a tall cleric, the Cardinal Inquisitor, who is

*accompanied by an astronomer. Galileo bows. Before going out he
whispers a question to the guard at the door.*

GUARD *whispers back*: His Eminence the Cardinal Inquisitor.
The astronomer leads the Cardinal Inquisitor up to the telescope.

7

But the Inquisition puts Copernicus's teachings on the Index (March 5th, 1616)

When Galileo was in Rome
A cardinal asked him to his home.
He wined and dined him as his guest
And only made one small request.

*Cardinal Bellarmin's house in Rome. A ball is in progress. In the
vestibule, where two clerical secretaries are playing chess and making
notes about the guests, Galileo is received with applause by a small
group of masked ladies and gentlemen. He arrives accompanied by his
daughter Virginia and her fiancé Ludovico Marsili.*

VIRGINIA: I'm not dancing with anybody else, Ludovico.
LUDOVICO: Your shoulder-strap's undone.
GALILEO:
Fret not, daughter, if perchance
You attract a wanton glance.
The eyes that catch a trembling lace
Will guess the heartbeat's quickened pace.
Lovely woman still may be
Careless with felicity.
VIRGINIA: Feel my heart.
GALILEO *puts his hand on her heart*: It's thumping.
VIRGINIA: I'd like to look beautiful.

GALILEO: You'd better, or they'll go back to wondering whether it turns or not.

LUDOVICO: Of course it doesn't turn. *Galileo laughs.* Rome is talking only of you. But after tonight, sir, they will be talking about your daughter.

GALILEO: It's supposed to be easy to look beautiful in the Roman spring. Even I shall start looking like an overweight Adonis. *To the secretaries*: I am to wait here for his Eminence the Cardinal. *To the couple*: Go off and enjoy yourselves. *Before they leave for the ball offstage Virginia again comes running back.*

VIRGINIA: Father, the hairdresser in the Via del Trionfo took me first, and he made four other ladies wait. He knew your name right away. *Exit.*

GALILEO *to the secretaries as they play chess*: How can you go on playing old-style chess? Cramped, cramped. Nowadays the play is to let the chief pieces roam across the whole board. The rooks like this – *he demonstrates* – and the bishops like that and the Queen like this and that. That way you have enough space and can plan ahead.

FIRST SECRETARY: It wouldn't go with our small salaries, you know. We can only do moves like this. *He makes a small move.*

GALILEO: You've got it wrong, my friend, quite wrong. If you live grandly enough you can afford to sweep the board. One has to move with the times, gentlemen. Not just hugging the coasts; sooner or later one has to venture out. *The very old cardinal from the previous scene crosses the stage, led by his monk. He notices Galileo, walks past him, turns round hesitantly and greets him. Galileo sits down. From the ballroom boys' voices are heard singing Lorenzo di Medici's famous poem on transience,*

I who have seen the summer's roses die
And all their petals pale and shrivelled lie

Upon the chilly ground, I know the truth:
How evanescent is the flower of youth.

GALILEO: Rome – A large party?

THE FIRST SECRETARY: The first carnival since the plague years. All Italy's great families are represented here tonight. The Orsinis, the Villanis, the Nuccolis, the Soldanieris, the Canes, the Lecchis, the d'Estes, the Colombinis . . .

SECOND SECRETARY *interrupting*: Their Eminences Cardinals Bellarmin and Barberini.

Enter Cardinal Bellarmin and Cardinal Barberini. They are holding sticks with the masks of a lamb and a dove over their faces.

BARBERINI *pointing at Galileo*: 'The sun also ariseth, and the sun goeth down, and hasteth to his place where he arose.' So says Solomon, and what does Galileo say?

GALILEO: When I was so high – *he indicates with his hand* – your Eminence, I stood on a ship and called out 'The shore is moving away.' Today I realise that the shore was standing still and the ship moving away.

BARBERINI: Ingenious, ingenious – what our eyes see, Bellarmin, in other words the rotation of the starry heavens, is not necessarily true – witness the ship and the shore. But what is true – i.e. the rotation of the earth – cannot be perceived. Ingenious. But his moons of Jupiter are a tough nut for our astronomers to crack. Unfortunately I once studied some astronomy, Bellarmin. It sticks to you like the itch.

BELLARMIN: We must move with the times, Barberini. If new star charts based on a new hypothesis help our mariners to navigate, then they should make use of them. We only disapprove of such doctrines as run counter to the Scriptures.

He waves toward the ballroom in greeting.

GALILEO: The Scriptures . . . 'He that withholdeth corn, the people shall curse him.' Proverbs of Solomon.

BARBERINI: 'A prudent man concealeth knowledge.' Proverbs of Solomon.

GALILEO: 'Where no oxen are the crib is clean: but much increase is by the strength of the ox.'

BARBERINI: 'He that ruleth his spirit is better than he that taketh a city.'

GALILEO: 'But a broken spirit drieth the bones.' *Pause*. 'Doth not wisdom cry?'

BARBERINI: 'Can one go upon hot coals, and his feet not be burned?' – Welcome to Rome, Galileo my friend. You know its origins? Two little boys, so runs the legend, were given milk and shelter by a she-wolf. Since that time all her children have had to pay for their milk. The she-wolf makes up for it by providing every kind of pleasure, earthly and heavenly, ranging from conversations with my friend Bellarmin to three or four ladies of international repute; let me point them out to you ...

He takes Galileo upstage to show him the ballroom. Galileo follows reluctantly.

BARBERINI: No? He would rather have a serious discussion. Right. Are you sure, Galileo my friend, that you astronomers aren't merely out to make astronomy simpler for yourselves? *He leads him forward once more.* You think in circles and ellipses and constant velocities, simple motions such as are adapted to your brains. Suppose it had pleased God to make his stars move like this? *With his finger he traces an extremely complicated course at an uneven speed.* What would that do to your calculations?

GALILEO: Your Eminence, if God had constructed the world like that – *he imitates Barberini's course* – then he would have gone on to construct our brains like that, so that they would regard such motions as the simplest. I believe in men's reason.

BARBERINI: I think men's reason is not up to the job.

Silence. He's too polite to go on and say he thinks mine is not up to the job.

Laughs and walks back to the balustrade.

BELLARMIN: Men's reason, my friend, does not take us very far. All around us we see nothing but crookedness, crime and weakness. Where is truth?

GALILEO *angrily*: I believe in men's reason.

BARBERINI *to the secretaries*: You needn't take this down; it's a scientific discussion among friends.

BELLARMIN: Think for an instant how much thought and effort it cost the Fathers of the Church and their countless successors to put some sense into this appalling world of ours. Think of the brutality of the landowners in the Campagna who have their half-naked peasants flogged to work, and of the stupidity of those poor people who kiss their feet in return.

GALILEO: Horrifying. As I was driving here I saw . . .

BELLARMIN: We have shifted the responsibility for such occurrences as we cannot understand – life is made up of them – to a higher Being, and argued that all of them contribute to the fulfilment of certain intentions, that the whole thing is taking place according to a great plan. Admittedly this hasn't satisfied everybody, but now you come along and accuse this higher Being of not being quite clear how the stars move, whereas you yourself are. Is that sensible?

GALILEO *starts to make a statement*: I am a faithful son of the Church . . .

BARBERINI: He's a terrible man. He cheerfully sets out to convict God of the most elementary errors in astronomy. I suppose God hadn't got far enough in his studies before he wrote the bible; is that it? My *dear* fellow . . .

BELLARMIN: Wouldn't you also think it possible that the Creator had a better idea of what he was making than those he has created?

GALILEO: But surely, gentlemen, mankind may not only get the motions of the stars wrong but the Bible too?

BELLARMIN: But isn't interpreting the Bible the business of Holy Church and her theologians, wouldn't you say? *Galileo is silent.*

BELLARMIN: You have no answer to that, have you? *He makes a sign to the secretaries*: Mr Galilei, tonight the Holy Office decided that the doctrine of Copernicus, according to which the sun is motionless and at the centre of the cosmos, while the earth moves and is not at the centre of the cosmos, is foolish, absurd, heretical and contrary to our faith. I have been charged to warn you that you must abandon this view.

GALILEO: What does this mean?

From the ballroom boys can be heard singing a further verse of the madrigal:

> I said: This lovely springtime cannot last
> So pluck your roses before May is past.

Barberini gestures Galileo not to speak till the song is finished. They listen.

GALILEO: And the facts? I understand that the Collegium Romanum had approved my observations.

BELLARMIN: And expressed their complete satisfaction, in terms very flattering to you.

GALILEO: But the moons of Jupiter, the phases of Venus . . .

BELLARMIN: The Holy Congregation took its decision without going into such details.

GALILEO: In other words, all further scientific research . . .

BELLARMIN: Is explicitly guaranteed, Mr Galilei. In line with the Church's view that it is impossible for us to know, but legitimate for us to explore. *He again greets a guest in the ballroom.* You are also at liberty to treat the doctrine in question mathematically, in the form of a hypothesis. Science is the rightful and much-loved daughter of the

Church, Mr Galilei. None of us seriously believes that you want to shake men's faith in the Church.

GALILEO *angrily*: What destroys faith is invoking it.

BARBERINI: Really? *He slaps him on the shoulder with a roar of laughter. Then he gives him a keen look and says in a not unfriendly manner*: Don't tip the baby out with the bathwater, Galileo my friend. *We* shan't. We need you more than you need us.

BELLARMIN: I cannot wait to introduce Italy's greatest mathematician to the Commissioner of the Holy Office, who has the highest possible esteem for you.

BARBERINI *taking Galileo's other arm.*: At which he turns himself back into a lamb. You too, my dear fellow, ought really to have come disguised as a good orthodox thinker. It's my own mask that permits me certain freedoms today. Dressed like this I might be heard to murmur: If God didn't exist we should have to invent him. Right, let's put on our masks once more. Poor old Galileo hasn't got one. *They put Galileo between them and escort him into the ballroom.*

FIRST SECRETARY: Did you get that last sentence?

SECOND SECRETARY: Just doing it. *They write rapidly.* Have you got that bit where he said he believes in men's reason? *Enter the Cardinal Inquisitor.*

THE INQUISITOR: Did the conversation take place?

FIRST SECRETARY *mechanically*: To start with Mr Galilei arrived with his daughter. She has become engaged today to Mr ... *The Inquisitor gestures him not to go on.* Mr Galilei then told us about the new way of playing chess in which, contrary to all the rules, the pieces are moved right across the board.

THE INQUISITOR *with a similar gesture*: The transcript. *A secretary hands him the transcripts and the cardinal sits down and skims through it. Two young ladies in masks cross the stage; they curtsey to the cardinal.*

ONE YOUNG LADY: Who's that?

THE OTHER: The Cardinal Inquisitor.

They giggle and go off. Enter Virginia, looking around for something.

THE INQUISITOR *from his corner*: Well, my daughter?

VIRGINIA *gives a slight start, not having seen him*: Oh, your Eminence . . .

Without looking up, the Inquisitor holds out his right hand to her. She approaches, kneels and kisses his ring.

THE INQUISITOR: A splendid night. Permit me to congratulate you on your engagement. Your future husband comes from a distinguished family. Are you staying long in Rome?

VIRGINIA: Not this time, your Eminence. A wedding takes so much preparing.

THE INQUISITOR: Ah, then you'll be returning to Florence like your father. I am glad of that. I expect that your father needs you. Mathematics is not the warmest of companions in the home, is it? Having a creature of flesh and blood around makes all the difference. It's easy to get lost in the world of the stars, with its immense distances, if one is a great man.

VIRGINIA *breathlessly*: You are very kind, your Eminence. I really understand practically nothing about such things.

THE INQUISITOR: Indeed? *He laughs*. In the fisherman's house no one eats fish, eh? It will tickle your father to hear that almost all your knowledge about the world of the stars comes ultimately from me, my child. *Leafing through the transcript*: It says here that our innovators, whose acknowledged leader is your father – a great man, one of the greatest – consider our present ideas about the significance of the dear old earth to be a little exaggerated. Well, from Ptolemy's time – and he was a wise man of antiquity – up to the present day we used to reckon that the whole of creation – in other words the entire crystal ball at whose centre the earth lies – measured about twenty thousand diametres of the earth across. Nice and roomy, but not large enough for innovators. Apparently they feel that it is unimaginably far-flung and that the earth's distance from the sun – quite a respectable distance, we always found it – is so minute compared with its distance from the fixed stars on the outermost sphere that our calculations can simply ignore it. Yes, our innovators are living on a very grand scale.

Virginia laughs. So does the Inquisitor.

THE INQUISITOR: True enough, there are a few gentlemen of the Holy Office who have started objecting, as it were, to such a view of the world, compared with which our picture so far has been a little miniature such as one might hang round the neck of certain young ladies. What worries them is that a prelate or even a cardinal might get lost in such vast distances and the Almighty might lose sight of the Pope himself. Yes, it's very amusing, but I am glad to know that you will remain close to your great father whom we all esteem so highly, my dear child. By the way, do I know your Father Confessor . . . ?

VIRGINIA: Father Christophorus of Saint Ursula.

THE INQUISITOR: Ah yes, I am glad that you will be going with your father. He will need you; perhaps you cannot imagine this, but the time will come. You are still so young and so very much flesh and blood, and greatness is occasionally a difficult burden for those on whom God has bestowed it; it can be. No mortal is so great that he cannot be contained in a prayer. But I am keeping you, my dear child, and I'll be making your fiancé jealous and maybe your father too by telling you something about the stars which is possibly out of date. Run off and dance; only mind you remember me to Father Christophorus.

Virginia makes a deep bow and goes.

8

A conversation

> Galileo, feeling grim,
> A young monk came to visit him.
> The monk was born of common folk.
> It was of science that they spoke.

In the Florentine Ambassador's palace in Rome Galileo is listening to the little monk who whispered the papal astronomer's remark to him after the meeting of the Collegium Romanum.

GALILEO: Go on, go on. The habit you're wearing gives you the right to say whatever you want.

THE LITTLE MONK: I studied mathematics, Mr Galilei.

GALILEO: That might come in handy if it led you to admit that two and two sometimes makes four.

THE LITTLE MONK: Mr Galilei, I have been unable to sleep for three days. I couldn't see how to reconcile the decree I had read with the moons of Jupiter which I had observed. Today I decided to say an early mass and come to you.

GALILEO: In order to tell me Jupiter has no moons?

THE LITTLE MONK: No. I have managed to see the wisdom of the decree. It has drawn my attention to the potential dangers for humanity in wholly unrestricted research, and I have decided to give astronomy up. But I also wanted to explain to you the motives which can make even an astronomer renounce pursuing that doctrine any further.

GALILEO: I can assure you that such motives are familiar to me.

THE LITTLE MONK: I understand your bitterness. You have in mind certain exceptional powers of enforcement at the Church's disposal.

GALILEO: Just call them instruments of torture.

THE LITTLE MONK: But I am referring to other motives. Let me speak about myself. My parents were peasants in the Campagna, and I grew up there. They are simple people. They know all about olive trees, but not much else. As I study the phases of Venus I can visualise my parents sitting round the fire with my sister, eating their curded cheese. I see the beams above them, blackened by hundreds of years of smoke, and I see every detail of their old worn hands and the little spoons they are holding. They are badly off, but even their misfortunes imply a certain order. There are so many cycles, ranging from washing the floor, through the seasons of the olive crop to the paying of taxes. There is a regularity about the disasters that befall them. My father's back does not get bent all at once, but more and more each spring he spends in the olive groves; just as the successive childbirths that have made my mother increasingly sexless have followed well-defined intervals. They draw the strength they need to carry their baskets sweating up the stony tracks, to bear children and even to eat, from the feeling of stability and necessity that comes of looking at the soil, at the annual greening of the trees and at the little church, and of listening to the bible passages read there every Sunday. They have been assured that God's eye is always on them – probingly, even anxiously –: that the whole drama of the world is constructed around them so that they, the performers, may prove themselves in their greater or lesser roles. What would my people say if I told them that they happen to be on a small knob of stone twisting endlessly through the void round a second-rate star, just one among myriads? What would be the value or necessity then of so much patience, such understanding of their own poverty? What would be the use of Holy Scripture, which has explained and justified it all – the sweat, the patience, the hunger, the submissiveness – and now

turns out to be full of errors? No: I can see their eyes
wavering, I can see them letting their spoons drop, I can
see how betrayed and deceived they will feel. So nobody's
eye is on us, they'll say. Have we got to look after ourselves, old, uneducated and worn-out as we are? The
only part anybody has devised for us is this wretched,
earthly one, to be played out on a tiny star wholly de-
pendent on others, with nothing revolving round it. Our
poverty has no meaning: hunger is no trial of strength, it's
merely not having eaten: effort is no virtue, it's just bending
and carrying. Can you see now why I read into the Holy
Congregations decree a noble motherly compassion; a vast
goodness of soul?

GALILEO: Goodness of soul! Aren't you really saying that
there's nothing for them, the wine has all been drunk, their
lips are parched, so they had better kiss the cassock? Why is
there nothing for them? Why does order in this country
mean the orderliness of a bare cupboard, and necessity
nothing but the need to work oneself to death? When there
are teeming vineyards and cornfields on every side? Your
Campagna peasants are paying for the wars which the
representative of gentle Jesus is waging in Germany and
Spain. Why does he make the earth the centre of the
universe? So that the See of St Peter can be the centre of the
earth! That's what it is all about. You're right, it's not about
the planets, it's about the peasants of the Campagna. And
don't talk to me about the beauty given to phenomena by
the patina of age! You know how the Margaritifera oyster
produces its pearl? By a mortally dangerous disease which
involves taking some unassimilable foreign body, like a
grain of sand, and wrapping it in a slimy ball. The process
all but kills it. To hell with the pearl, give me the healthy
oyster. Virtues are not an offshoot of poverty, my dear
fellow. If your people were happy and prosperous they
could develop the virtues of happiness and prosperity. At

present the virtues of exhaustion derive from exhausted fields, and I reject them. Sir, my new pumps will perform more miracles in that direction than all your ridiculous superhuman slaving. – 'Be fruitful and multiply', since your fields are not fruitful and you are being decimated by wars. Am I supposed to tell your people lies?

THE LITTLE MONK *much agitated*: We have the highest of all motives for keeping our mouths shut – the peace of mind of the less fortunate.

GALILEO: Would you like me to show you a Cellini clock that Cardinal Bellarmin's coachman brought round this morning? My dear fellow, authority is rewarding me for not disturbing the peace of mind of people like your parents, by offering me the wine they press in the sweat of their countenance which we all know to have been made in God's image. If I were to agree to keep my mouth shut my motives would be thoroughly low ones: an easy life, freedom from persecution, and so on.

THE LITTLE MONK: Mr Galilei, I am a priest.

GALILEO: You're also a physicist. And you can see that Venus has phases. Here, look out there! *He points at the window*. Can you see the little Priapus on the fountain next the laurel bush? The god of gardens, birds and thieves, rich in two thousand years of bucolic indecency. Even he was less of a liar. All right, let's drop it. I too am a son of the Church. But do you know the eighth Satire of Horace? I've been rereading it again lately, it acts as a kind of counterweight. *He picks up a small book*. He makes his Priapus speak – a little statue which was then in the Esquiline gardens. Starting:

> Stump of a figtree, useless kind of wood
> Was I once; then the carpenter, not sure
> Whether to make a Priapus or a stool
> Opted for the god . . .

Can you imagine Horace being told not to mention stools and agreeing to put a table in the poem instead? Sir, it offends my sense of beauty if my cosmogony has a Venus without phases. We cannot invent mechanisms to pump water up from rivers if we are not to be allowed to study the greatest of all mechanisms right under our nose, that of the heavenly bodies. The sum of the angles in a triangle cannot be varied to suit the Vatican's convenience. I can't calculate the courses of flying bodies in such a way as also to explain witches taking trips on broomsticks.

THE LITTLE MONK: But don't you think that the truth will get through without us, so long as it's true?

GALILEO: No, no, no. The only truth that gets through will be what we force through: the victory of reason will be the victory of people who are prepared to reason, nothing else. Your picture of the Campagna peasants makes them look like the moss on their own huts. How can anyone imagine that the sum of the angles in a triangle conflicts with *their* needs? But unless they get moving and learn how to think, they will find even the finest irrigation systems won't help them. Oh, to hell with it: I see your people's divine patience, but where is their divine anger?

THE LITTLE MONK: They are tired.

GALILEO *tosses him a bundle of manuscripts*: Are you a physicist, my son? Here you have the reasons why the ocean moves, ebbing and flowing. But you're not supposed to read it, d'you hear? Oh, you've already started. You are a physicist, then? *The little monk is absorbed in the papers.*

GALILEO: An apple from the tree of knowledge! He's wolfing it down. He is damned for ever, but he has got to wolf it down, the poor glutton. I sometimes think I'll have myself shut up in a dungeon ten fathoms below ground in complete darkness if only it will help me to find out what light is. And the worst thing is that what I know I have to tell people, like a lover, like a drunkard, like a traitor. It is

an absolute vice and leads to disaster. How long can I go on
shouting it into the void, that's the question.

THE LITTLE MONK *indicating a passage in the papers*: I don't
understand this sentence.

GALILEO: I'll explain it you, I'll explain it to you.

9

After keeping silent for eight years, Galileo is en-
couraged by the accession of a new pope, himself
a scientist, to resume his researches into the forbidden area: the sunspots

> Eight long years with tongue in cheek
> Of what he knew he did not speak.
> Then temptation grew too great
> And Galileo challenged fate.

*Galileo's house in Florence. Galileo's pupils – Federzoni, the little
monk and Andrea Sarti, a young man now – have gathered to see an
experiment demonstrated. Galileo himself is standing reading a book.
Virginia and Mrs Sarti are sewing her trousseau.*

VIRGINIA: Sewing one's trousseau is fun. That one's for
entertaining at the long table; Ludovico likes entertaining.
It's got to be neat, though; his mother can spot every loose
thread. She doesn't like Father's books. Nor does Father
Christophorus.

MRS SARTI: He hasn't written a book for years.

VIRGINIA: I think he realises he was wrong. A very high
church person in Rome told me a lot about astronomy. The
distances are too great.

ANDREA *writing the day's programme on the board*: 'Thursday
p.m. Floating bodies' – as before, ice, bucket of water,
balance, iron needle, Aristotle.

He fetches these things. The others are reading books.
Enter Filippo Mucius, a scholar in middle age. He appears some-
what distraught.

MUCIUS: Could you tell Mr Galilei that he has got to see me?
He is condemning me unheard.

MRS SARTI: But he won't receive you.

MUCIUS: God will recompense you if you will only ask. I
must speak to him.

VIRGINIA *goes to the stairs*: Father!

GALILEO: What is it?

VIRGINIA: Mr Mucius.

GALILEO *looking up sharply, goes to the head of the stairs, followed
by his pupils*: What do you want?

MUCIUS: Mr Galilei, may I be allowed to explain those
passages from my book which seem to contain a condemnation of Copernicus's theories about the rotation of the
earth? I have . . .

GALILEO: What do you want to explain? You are fully in
line with the Holy Congregation's decree of 1616. You cannot be faulted. You did of course study mathematics here,
but that's no reason why we should need to hear you
say that two and two makes four. You are quite within your
rights in saying that this stone – *he takes a little stone from his
pocket and throws it down to the hall* – has just flown up to the
ceiling.

MUCIUS: Mr Galilei, I . . .

GALILEO: Don't talk to me about difficulties. I didn't let
the plague stop me from recording my observations.

MUCIUS: Mr Galilei, there are worse things than the plague.

GALILEO: Listen to me: someone who doesn't know the
truth is just thick-headed. But someone who does know it
and calls it a lie is a crook. Get out of my house.

MUCIUS *tonelessly*: You're quite right.

He goes out.
Galileo goes back into his work room.

FEDERZONI: Too bad. He's not a great man and no one would take him seriously for one moment if he hadn't been your pupil. Now of course people are saying 'he's heard everything Galileo had to teach and he's forced to admit that it's all nonsense'.

MRS SARTI: I'm sorry for the poor gentleman.

VIRGINIA: Father was too good to him.

MRS SARTI: I really wanted to talk to you about your marriage, Virginia. You're such a child still, and got no mother, and your father keeps putting those little bits of ice on water. Anyhow I wouldn't ask him anything to do with your marriage if I were you. He'd keep on for days saying the most dreadful things, preferably at meals and when the young people are there, because he hasn't got half a scudo's worth of shame in his make-up, and never had. But I'm not talking about that kind of thing, just about how the future will turn out. Not that I'm in a position to know anything myself. I'm not educated. But nobody goes blindly into a serious affair like this. I really think you ought to go to a proper astronomer at the university and get him to cast your horoscope so you know what you're in for. Why are you laughing?

VIRGINIA: Because I've been.

MRS SARTI *very inquisitive*: What did he say?

VIRGINIA: For three months I'll have to be careful, because the sun will be in Aries, but then I shall get a particularly favourable ascendant and the clouds will part. So long as I keep my eye on Jupiter I can travel as much as I like, because I'm an Aries.

MRS SARTI: And Ludovico?

VIRGINIA: He's a Leo. *After a little pause*: That's supposed to be sensual. *Pause*

VIRGINIA: I know whose step that is. It's Mr Gaffone, the Rector.

Enter Mr Gaffone, Rector of the University.

GAFFONE: I'm just bringing a book which I think might interest your father. For heaven's sake please don't disturb him. I can't help it; I always feel that every moment stolen from that great man is a moment stolen from Italy. I'll lay it neatly and daintily in your hands and slip away, on tiptoe. *He goes. Virginia gives the book to Federzoni.*

GALILEO: What's it about?

FEDERZONI: I don't know. *Spelling out*: 'De maculis in sole'.

ANDREA: About sunspots. Yet another.

Federzoni irritably passes it on to him.

ANDREA: Listen to the dedication. 'To the greatest living authority on physics, Galileo Galilei.'

Galileo is once more deep in his book.

ANDREA: I've read the treatise on sunspots which Fabricius has written in Holland. He thinks they are clusters of stars passing between the earth and the sun.

THE LITTLE MONK: Doubtful, don't you think, Mr Galilei?

Galileo does not answer.

ANDREA: In Paris and in Prague they think they are vapours from the sun.

FEDERZONI: Hm.

ANDREA: Federzoni doubts it.

FEDERZONI: Leave me out of it, would you? I said 'Hm', that's all. I'm your lensgrinder, I grind lenses and you make observations of the sky through them and what you see isn't spots but 'maculis'. How am I to doubt anything? How often do I have to tell you I can't read the books, they're in Latin? *In his anger he gesticulates with the scales. One of the pans falls to the floor. Galileo goes over and picks it up without saying anything.*

THE LITTLE MONK: There's happiness in doubting: I wonder why.

ANDREA: Every sunny day for the past two weeks I've gone up to the attic, under the roof. The narrow chinks between the shingles let just a thin ray of light through. If you take a sheet of paper you can catch the sun's image upside down. I saw a spot as big as a fly, as smudged as a cloud. It was moving. Why aren't we investigating those spots, Mr Galilei?

GALILEO: Because we're working on floating bodies.

ANDREA: Mother's got great baskets full of letters. The whole of Europe wants to know what you think, you've such a reputation now, you can't just say nothing.

GALILEO: Rome allowed me to get a reputation because I said nothing.

FEDERZONI: But you can't afford to go on saying nothing now.

GALILEO: Nor can I afford to be roasted over a wood fire like a ham.

ANDREA: Does that mean you think the sunspots are part of this business?

Galileo does not answer.

ANDREA: All right, let's stick to our bits of ice, they can't hurt you.

GALILEO: Correct. – Our proposition, Andrea?

ANDREA: As for floating, we assume that it depends not on a body's form but on whether it is lighter or heavier than water.

GALILEO: What does Aristotle say?

THE LITTLE MONK: 'Discus latus platique . . .'

GALILEO: For God's sake translate it.

THE LITTLE MONK: 'A broad flat piece of ice will float on water whereas an iron needle will sink.'

GALILEO: Why does the ice not sink, in Aristotle's view?

THE LITTLE MONK: Because it is broad and flat and therefore cannot divide the water.

GALILEO: Right. *He takes a piece of ice and places it in the bucket.* Now I am pressing the ice hard against the bottom of the bucket. I release the pressure of my hands. What happens?

THE LITTLE MONK: It shoots up to the top again.

GALILEO: Correct. Apparently it can divide the water all right as it rises. Fulganzio!

THE LITTLE MONK: But why can it float in the first place? It's heavier than water, because it is concentrated water.

GALILEO: Suppose it were thinned-down water?

ANDREA: It has to be lighter than water, or it wouldn't float.

GALILEO: Aha.

ANDREA: Any more than an iron needle can float. Everything lighter than water floats and everything heavier sinks. QED.

GALILEO: Andrea, you must learn to think cautiously. Hand me the needle. A sheet of paper. Is iron heavier than water?

ANDREA: Yes.

Galileo lays the needle on a piece of paper and launches it on the water. A pause.

GALILEO: What happens?

FEDERZONI: The needle's floating. Holy Aristotle, they never checked up on him!

They laugh.

GALILEO: One of the main reasons why the sciences are so poor is that they imagine they are so rich. It isn't their job to throw open the door to infinite wisdom but to put a limit to infinite error. Make your notes.

VIRGINIA: What is it?

MRS SARTI: Whenever they laugh it gives me a turn. What are they laughing about, I ask myself.

VIRGINIA: Father says theologians have their bells to ring: physicists have their laughter.

MRS SARTI: Anyway I'm glad he isn't looking through his tube so often these days. That was even worse.

VIRGINIA: All he's doing now is put bits of ice in water: that can't do much harm.

MRS SARTI: I don't know.

Enter Ludovico Marsili in travelling clothes, followed by a servant carrying items of luggage. Virginia runs up and throws her arms round him.

VIRGINIA: Why didn't you write and say you were coming?

LUDOVICO: I happened to be in the area, inspecting our vineyards at Buccioli, and couldn't resist the chance.

GALILEO *as though short-sighted*: Who is it?

VIRGINIA: Ludovico.

THE LITTLE MONK: Can't you see him?

GALILEO: Ah yes, Ludovico. *Goes towards him.* How are the horses?

LUDOVICO: Doing fine, sir.

GALILEO: Sarti, we're celebrating. Get us a jug of that Sicilian wine, the old sort.

Exit Mrs Sarti with Andrea.

LUDOVICO *to Virginia*: You look pale. Country life will suit you. My mother is expecting you in September.

VIRGINIA: Wait a moment, I'll show you my wedding dress. *Runs out.*

GALILEO: Sit down.

LUDOVICO: I'm told there are over a thousand students going to your lectures at the university, sir. What are you working at just now?

GALILEO: Routine stuff. Did you come through Rome?

LUDOVICO: Yes. – Before I forget: my mother congratulates you on your remarkable tact in connection with those sun-sport orgies the Dutch have been going in for lately.

GALILEO *drily*: Very kind of her.

Mrs Sarti and Andrea bring wine and glasses. Everyone gathers round the table.

LUDOVICO: I can tell you what all the gossip will be about in Rome this February. Christopher Clavius said he's afraid the whole earth-round-the-sun act will start up again because of these sunspots.

ANDREA: No chance.

GALILEO: Any other news from the Holy City, aside from hopes of fresh lapses on my part?

LUDOVICO: I suppose you know that His Holiness is dying?

THE LITTLE MONK: Oh.

GALILEO: Who do they think will succeed him?

LUDOVICO: The favourite is Barberini.

GALILEO: Barberini.

ANDREA: Mr Galilei knows Barberini.

THE LITTLE MONK: Cardinal Barberini is a mathematician.

FEDERZONI: A scientist at the Holy See!

Pause.

GALILEO: Well: so now they need people like Barberini who have read a bit of mathematics! Things are beginning to move. Federzoni, we may yet see the day when we no longer have to look over our shoulder like criminals every time we say two and two equals four. *To Ludovico*: I like this wine, Ludovico. What do you think of it?

LUDOVICO: It's good.

GALILEO: I know the vineyard. The hillside is steep and stony, the grapes almost blue. I love this wine.

LUDOVOCI: Yes, sir.

GALILEO: It has got little shadows in it. And it is almost sweet but just stops short of it. – Andrea, clear all that stuff away, the ice, needle and bucket. – I value the consolations of the flesh. I've no use for those chicken-hearts who see them as weaknesses. Pleasure takes some achieving, I'd say.

THE LITTLE MONK: What have you in mind?

FEDERZONI: We're starting up the earth-round-the-sun act again.

ANDREA *hums*:

It's fixed, the Scriptures say. And so
Orthodox science proves.
The Holy Father grabs its ears, to show
It's firmly held. And yet it moves.

Andrea, Federzoni and the little monk hurry to the work table and clear it.

ANDREA: We might find that the sun goes round too. How would that suit you, Marsili?

LUDOVICO: What's the excitement about?

MRS SARTI: You're not going to start up that devilish business again, surely, Mr Galilei?

GALILEO: Now I know why your mother sent you to me. Barberini in the ascendant! Knowledge will become a passion and research an ecstasy. Clavius is right, those sunspots interest me. Do you like my wine, Ludovico?

LUDOVICO: I told you I did, Sir.

GALILEO: You really like it?

LUDOVICO *stiffly*: I like it.

GALILEO: Would you go so far as to accept a man's wine or his daughter without asking him to give up his profession? What has my astronomy got to do with my daughter? The phases of Venus can't alter my daughter's backside.

MRS SARTI: Don't be so vulgar. I am going to fetch Virginia.

LUDOVICO *holding her back*: Marriages in families like ours are not based on purely sexual considerations.

GALILEO: Did they stop you from marrying my daughter for eight years because I had a term of probation to serve?

LUDOVICO: My wife will also have to take her place in our pew in the village church.

GALILEO: You think your peasants will go by the saintliness of their mistress in deciding whether to pay rent or not?

LUDOVICO: In a sense, yes.

GALILEO: Andrea, Fulganzio, get out the brass reflector and the screen! We will project the sun's image on it so as to protect our eyes; that's your method, Andrea.

Andrea and the little monk fetch reflector and screen.

LUDOVICO: You did sign a declaration in Rome, you know, Sir, saying you would have nothing more to do with this earth-round-the-sun business.

GALILEO: Oh that. In those days we had a reactionary pope.

MRS SARTI: Had! And his Holiness not even dead yet!

GALILEO: Almost. Put a grid of squares on the screen. We will do this methodically. And then we'll be able to answer their letters, won't we, Andrea?

MRS SARTI: 'Almost' indeed. The man'll weigh his pieces of ice fifty times over, but as soon as it's something that suits his book he believes it blindly.

The screen is set up.

LUDOVICO: If His Holiness does die, Mr Galilei, irrespective who the next pope is and how intense his devotion to the sciences, he will also have to take into account the devotion felt for him by the most respected families in the land.

THE LITTLE MONK: God made the physical world, Ludovico; God made the human brain; God will permit physics.

MRS SARTI: Galileo, I am going to say something to you. I have watched my son slipping into sin with all those 'experiments' and 'theories' and 'observations' and there was nothing I could do about it. You set yourself up against the authorities and they have already warned you once. The highest cardinals spoke to you like to a sick horse. That worked for a time, but then two months ago, just after the Feast of the Immaculate Conception, I caught you secretly starting your 'observations' again. In the attic. I didn't say much but I knew what to do. I ran and lit a candle to St Joseph. It's more than I can cope with. When I get you on your own you show vestiges of sense and tell me you know you've got to behave or else it'll be dangerous; but two days of experiments and you're just as bad as before. If I choose to forfeit eternal bliss by sticking with a heretic that's my business, but you have no right to trample all over your daughter's happiness with your great feet.

GALILEO *gruffly*: Bring the telescope.

LUDOVICO: Giuseppe, take our luggage back to the coach.

The servant goes out.

MRS SARTI: She'll never get over this. You can tell her yourself.

Hurries off, still carrying the jug.

LUDOVICO: I see you have made your preparations. Mr Galileo, my mother and I spend three quarters of each year on our estate in the Campagna, and we can assure you that our peasants are not disturbed by your papers on Jupiter and its moons. They are kept too busy in the fields. But they could be upset if they heard that frivolous attacks on the church's sacred doctrines were in future to go unpunished. Don't forget that the poor things are little better than animals and get everything muddled up. They are like beasts really, you can hardly imagine it. If rumour says a pear has been seen on an apple tree they will drop their work and hurry off to gossip about it.

GALILEO *interested*: Really?

LUDOVICO: Beasts. If they come up to the house to make some minor complaint or other, my mother is forced to have a dog whipped before their eyes, as the only way to recall them to discipline and order and a proper respect. You, Mr Galileo, may see rich cornfields from your coach as you pass, you eat our olives and our cheese, without a thought, and you have no idea how much trouble it takes to produce them, how much supervision.

GALILEO: Young man, I do not eat my olives without a thought. *Roughly*: You're holding me up. *Calls through the door*: Got the screen?

ANDREA: Yes. Are you coming?

GALILEO: Dogs aren't the only thing you whip to keep them in line, are they Marsili?

LUDOVICO: Mr Galileo. You have a marvellous brain. Pity.

THE LITTLE MONK *amazed*: He's threatening you.

GALILEO: Yes, I might stir up his peasants to think new thoughts. And his servants and his stewards.

FEDERZONI: How? None of them can read Latin.

GALILEO: I might write in the language of the people, for the many, rather than in Latin for the few. Our new thoughts call for people who work with their hands. Who else cares about knowing the causes of things? People who only see bread on their table don't want to know how it got baked; that lot would sooner thank God than thank the baker. But the people who make the bread will understand that nothing moves unless it has been made to move. Your sister pressing olives, Fulganzio, won't be astounded but will probably laugh when she hears that the sun isn't a golden coat of arms but a motor: that the earth moves because the sun sets it moving.

LUDOVICO: You will always be the slave of your passions. Make my excuses to Virginia; I think it will be better if I don't see her.

GALILEO: Her dowry will remain available to you, at any time.

LUDOVICO: Good day. *He goes.*

ANDREA: And our kindest regards to all the Marsilis.

FEDERZONI: Who command the earth to stand still so their castles shan't tumble down.

ANDREA: And the Cenzis and the Villanis!

FEDERZONI: The Cervillis!

ANDREA: The Lecchis!

FEDERZONI: The Pirleonis!

ANDREA: Who are prepared to kiss the pope's toe only if he uses it to kick the people with!

THE LITTLE MONK *likewise at the instruments*: The new pope is going to be an enlightened man.

GALILEO: So let us embark on the examination of those spots on the sun in which we are interested, at our own risk and without banking too much on the protection of a new pope.

ANDREA *interrupting*: But fully convinced that we shall dispel Mr Fabricius's star shadows along with the sun vapours of Paris and Prague, and establish the rotation of the sun.

GALILEO: Somewhat convinced that we shall establish the rotation of the sun. My object is not to establish that I was right but to find out if I am. Abandon hope, I say, all ye who enter on observation. They may be vapours, they may be spots, but before we assume that they are spots – which is what would suit us best – we should assume that they are fried fish. In fact we shall question everything all over again. And we shall go forward not in seven-league boots but at a snail's pace. And what we discover today we shall wipe off the slate tomorrow and only write it up again once we have again discovered it. And whatever we wish to find we shall regard, once found, with particular mistrust. So we shall approach the observation of the sun with an irrevocable determination to establish that the earth does *not* move. Only when we have failed, have been utterly and hopelessly beaten and are licking our wounds in the profoundest depression, shall we start asking if we weren't right after all, and the earth does go round. *With a twinkle*: But once every other hypothesis has crumbled in our hands then there will be no mercy for those who failed to research, and who go on talking all the same. Take the cloth off the telescope and point it at the sun!

He adjusts the brass reflector

THE LITTLE MONK: I knew you had begun working on this. I knew when you failed to recognise Mr Marsili.

In silence they begin their observations. As the sun's flaming image appears on the screen Virginia comes running in in her wedding dress.

VIRGINIA: You sent him away, father.

She faints. Andrea and the little monk hurry to her side.

GALILEO: I've got to know.

10

During the next decade Galileo's doctrine spreads among the common people. Ballad-singers and pamphleteers everywhere take up the new ideas. In the carnival of 1632 many Italian cities choose astronomy as the theme for their guilds' carnival processions

A half-starved couple of fairground people with a baby and a five-year old girl enter a market place where a partly masked crowd is awaiting the carnival procession. The two of them are carrying bundles, a drum and other utensils.

THE BALLAD SINGER *drumming*: Honoured inhabitants, ladies and gentlemen! To introduce the great carnival procession of the guilds we are going to perform the latest song from Florence which is now being sung all over north Italy and has been imported by us at vast expense. It is called: Ye horrible doctrine and opinions of Messer Galileo Galilei, physicist to the court, or A Foretaste of ye Future. *He sings*:

> When the Almighty made the universe
> He made the earth and then he made the sun.
> Then round the earth he bade the sun to turn –
> That's in the Bible, Genesis, Chapter One.
> And from that time all creatures here below
> Were in obedient circles meant to go.
>
> So the circles were all woven:
> Around the greater went the smaller
> Around the pace-setter the crawler
> On earth as it is in heaven.
> Around the pope the cardinals
> Around the cardinals the bishops

Around the bishops the secretaries
Around the secretaries the aldermen
Around the aldermen the craftsmen
Around the craftsmen the servants
Around the servants the dogs, the chickens and the
    beggars.

That, good people, is the Great Order of things, ordo
ordinum as the theologians call it, regula aeternis, the rule
of rules; but what, dear people, happened?
Sings:

Up stood the learned Galilei
(Chucked away the Bible, whipped out his telescope, took a
quick look at the universe.)
    And told the sun 'Stop there.
    From now the whole creatio dei
    Will turn as I think fair:
    The boss starts turning from today
    His servants stand and stare'.

    Now that's no joke, my friends, it is no matter small.
    Each day our servants' insolence increases
    But one thing's true, pleasures are few. I ask you all:
    Who wouldn't like to say and do just as he pleases?

Honourable inhabitants, such doctrines are utterly impossible.
He sings:

    The serf stays sitting on his arse.
    This turning's turned his head.
    The altar boy won't serve the mass
    The apprentice lies in bed.

    No, no, my friends, the Bible is no matter small
    Once let them off the lead indeed all loyalty ceases
    For one thing's true, pleasures are few. I ask you all:
    Who wouldn't like to say and do just as he pleases?

Good people all, kindly take a glance at the future as fore-
told by the learned Doctor Galileo Galilei:

Two housewives standing buying fish
Don't like the fish they're shown
The fishwife takes a hunk of bread
And eats them up alone.
The mason clears the building site
And hauls the builders' stone.
And when the house is finished quite
He keeps it as his own.

Can such things be my friends? It is no matter small
For independent spirit spreads like foul diseases.
But one thing's true, pleasures are few. I ask you all:
Who wouldn't like to say and do just as he pleases?

The tenant gives his landlord hell
Not caring in the least.
His wife now feeds her children well
On the milk she fed the priest.

No, no, my friends, the Bible is no matter small
Once let them off the lead indeed all loyalty ceases.
But one thing's true, pleasures are few. I ask you all:
Who wouldn't like to say and do just as he pleases?

THE SINGER'S WIFE:
I lately went a bit too far
And told my husband I'd see
If I could get some other fixed star
To do what he does for me.

BALLAD SINGER:
No, no, no, no, no, no! Stop, Galileo, stop.
Once take a mad dog's muzzle off it spreads diseases
People must keep their place, some down and some on
    top.
(Although it's nice for once to do just as one pleases).

BOTH:

> Good people who have trouble here below
> In serving cruel lords and gentle Jesus
> Who bid you turn the other cheek just so
> They're better placed to strike the second blow:
> Obedience isn't going to cure your woe
> So each of you wake up, and do just as he pleases!

THE BALLAD SINGER: Honoured inhabitants, you will now see Galileo Galilei's amazing discovery: the earth circling round the sun!

He belabours the drum violently. The woman and child step forward. The woman holds a crude image of the sun while the child, with a pumpkin over its head to represent the earth, circles round her. The singer points elatedly at the child as if it were performing a dangerous leap as it takes jerky steps to single beats on the drum. Then comes drumming from the rear.

A DEEP VOICE *calls*: The procession!

Enter two men in rags pulling a little cart. On an absurd throne sits the 'Grand-Duke of Florence', a figure with a cardboard crown dressed in sacking and looking through a telescope. Above his throne a sign saying 'Looking for trouble'. Then four masked men march in carrying a big tarpaulin. They stop and toss a puppet representing a cardinal into the air. A dwarf has taken up position to one side with a sign saying 'The new age'. In the crowd a beggar gets up on his crutches and dances, stamping the ground till he crashes to earth. Enter an over-lifesize puppet, Galileo Galilei, bowing to the audience. Before it goes a boy carrying a gigantic bible, open, with crossed-out pages.

THE BALLAD-SINGER: Galileo Galilei, the bible-buster!

Huge laughter among the crowd.

11

1633: The Inquisition summons the world-famous scientist to Rome

> The depths are hot, the heights are chill
> The streets are loud, the court is still.

Antechamber and staircase in the Medici palace in Florence. Galileo and his daughter are waiting to be admitted by the Grand Duke.

VIRGINIA: This is taking a long time.

GALILEO: Yes.

VIRGINIA: There's that fellow again who followed us here. *She points out an individual who walks past without looking at them.*

GALILEO *whose eyes have suffered*: I don't know him.

VIRGINIA: I've seen him several times in the past few days, though. He gives me the creeps.

GALILEO: Rubbish. We're in Florence, not among Corsican bandits.

VIRGINIA: Here's Rector Gaffone.

GALILEO: He makes me want to run. That idiot will involve me in another of his interminable talks.
Down the stairs comes Mr Gaffone, rector of the university. He is visibly alarmed on seeing Galileo and walks stiffly past them barely nodding, his head awkwardly averted.

GALILEO: What's got into the man? My eyes are bad again. Did he even greet us?

VIRGINIA: Barely. What's in your book? Could it be thought heretical maybe?

GALILEO: You're wasting too much time in church. You'll spoil what's left of your complexion with all this early rising and scurrying off to mass. You're praying for me, is that it?

VIRGINIA: Here's Mr Vanni the ironfounder you designed the furnace for. Don't forget to thank him for those quails. *A man has come down the stairs.*

VANNI: Were those good quails I sent you, Mr Galilei?

GALILEO: The quails were first-rate, Messer Vanni, many thanks again.

VANNI: Your name was mentioned upstairs. They're blaming you for those pamphlets against the bible that have been selling all over the place lately.

GALILEO: I know nothing about pamphlets. The Bible and Homer are my preferred reading.

VANNI: Even if that weren't so I'd like to take this chance to say that we manufacturers are behind you. I'm not the sort of fellow that knows much about the stars, but to me you're the man who's battling for freedom to teach what's new. Take that mechanical cultivator from Germany you were describing to me. In the past year alone five books on agriculture have been published in London. We'd be glad enough to have a book on the Dutch canals. The same sort of people as are trying to block you are stopping the Bologna doctors from dissecting bodies for medical research.

GALILEO: Your voice can be heard, Vanni.

VANNI: I should hope so. Do you realise that they've now got money markets in Amsterdam and London? Commercial schools too. Regularly printed papers with news in them. In this place we haven't even the freedom to make money. They're against ironfoundries because they imagine putting too many workers in one place leads to immorality. I sink or swim with people like you, Mr Galilei. If anybody ever tries launching anything against you, please remember you've friends in every branch of business. You've got the north Italian cities behind you, sir.

GALILEO: As far as I know nobody's thinking of launching anything against me.

VANNI: No?

GALILEO: No.

VANNI: I think you'd be better off in Venice. Fewer clerics. You could take up the cudgels from there. I've a travelling coach and horses, Mr Galilei.

GALILEO: I don't see myself as a refugee. I like my comforts.

VANNI: Surely. But from what I heard upstairs I'd say there was a hurry. It's my impression they'd be glad to know you weren't in Florence just now.

GALILEO: Nonsense. The Grand Duke is my pupil, and what's more the pope himself would never stand for any kind of attempt to trap me.

VANNI: I'm not sure you're good at distinguishing your friends from your enemies, Mr Galilei.

GALILEO: I can distinguish power from impotence. *He goes off brusquely.*

VANNI: Right. I wish you luck. *Exit.*

GALILEO *returning to Virginia*: Every local Tom, Dick and Harry with an axe to grind wants me to be his spokesman, particularly in places where it's not exactly helpful to me. I've written a book about the mechanics of the universe, that's all. What people make of it or don't make of it isn't my business.

VIRGINIA *loudly*: If they only knew how you condemned all those incidents at last carnival-time!

GALILEO: Yes. Give a bear honey and if the brute's hungry you risk losing your arm.

VIRGINIA *quietly*: Did the Grand Duke actually send for you today?

GALILEO: No, but I had myself announced. He wants to have the book, he has paid for it. Ask that official and tell him we don't like being kept waiting.

VIRGINIA *followed by the same individual, goes and addresses an official*: Mr Mincio, has his Highness been told my father wishes to speak with him?

THE OFFICIAL: How am I to know?

VIRGINIA: I don't call that an answer.

THE OFFICIAL: Don't you?

VIRGINIA: You're supposed to be polite.

The official half turns his back on her and yawns as he looks at the individual.

VIRGINIA *returning*: He says the Grand Duke is still busy.

GALILEO: I heard you say something about 'polite'. What was it?

VIRGINIA: I was thanking him for his polite answer, that's all. Can't you just leave the book here? You could use the time.

GALILEO: I'm beginning to wonder how much my time is worth. Perhaps I'll accept Sagredo's invitation to spend a few weeks in Padua after all. My health's not what it was.

VIRGINIA: You couldn't live without your books.

GALILEO: We could take a crate or two of that Sicilian wine in the coach with us.

VIRGINIA: You've always said it doesn't travel. And the court owes you three months' salary. They'll never forward it.

GALILEO: That's true.

The Cardinal Inquisitor comes down the stairs.

VIRGINIA: The Cardinal Inquisitor.

As he walks past he makes a deep bow to Galileo.

VIRGINIA: What's the Cardinal Inquisitor doing in Florence, Father?

GALILEO: I don't know. He behaved quite respectfully. I knew what I was doing when I came to Florence and kept quiet for all those years. They've paid me such tributes that now they're forced to accept me as I am.

THE OFFICIAL *calls out*: His Highness the Grand Duke!

Cosmo di Medici comes down the staircase. Galileo goes to meet him. Cosmo stops somewhat embarrassedly.

GALILEO: I wanted to bring my Dialogues on Two World Systems to your . . .

COSMO: Ah, yes. How are your eyes?

GALILEO: Not too good, your Highness. If your Highness permits, I have the book . . .

COSMO: The state of your eyes worries me. It worries me, truly. It shows me that you've been a little too eager to use that admirable tube of yours, haven't you?

He walks on without accepting the book.

GALILEO: He didn't take the book, did he?

VIRGINIA: Father, I'm scared.

GALILEO *firmly, in a low voice*: Control your feelings. We're not going home after this, we're going to Volpi the glazier's. I've fixed with him to have a cart full of empty barrels standing permanently in the yard of the winehouse next door, ready to take me out of the city.

VIRGINIA: So you knew . . .

GALILEO: Don't look round.

They start to go.

A HIGH OFFICIAL *comes down the stairs*: Mr Galilei, I have been charged to tell you that the court of Florence is no longer in a position to oppose the Holy Inquisition's wish to interrogate you in Rome. The coach of the Holy Inquisition awaits you, Mr Galilei.

12

The Pope

Room in the Vatican. Pope Urban VIII (formerly Cardinal Barberini) has received the Cardinal Inquisitor. In the course of the audience he is robed. Outside is heard the shuffling of many feet.

THE POPE *very loudly*: No! No! No!

THE INQUISITOR: So it is your Holiness's intention to go

before this gathering of doctors from every faculty, representatives of every order and the entire clergy, all with their naive faith in the word of God as set down in the scriptures, who are now assembling here to have that trust confirmed by your Holiness, and tell them that those scriptures can no longer be regarded as true?

THE POPE: I am not going to have the multiplication table broken. No!

THE INQUISITOR: Ah, it's the multiplication table, not the spirit of insubordination and doubt: that's what these people will tell you. But it isn't the multiplication table. No, a terrible restlessness has descended on the world. It is the restlessness of their own brain which these people have transferred to the unmoving earth. They shout 'But look at the figures'. But where do their figures come from? Everybody knows they originate in doubt. These people doubt everything. Are we to base human society on doubt and no longer on faith? 'You are my lord, but I doubt if that's a good thing'. 'This is your house and your wife, but I doubt if they shouldn't be mine.' Against that we have your Holiness's love of art, to which we owe our fine collections, being subjected to such disgraceful interpretations as we see scrawled on the walls of Roman houses: 'The Barberinis take what the Barbarians left.' And abroad? Your Holiness's Spanish policy has been misinterpreted by short-sighted critics, its antagonising of the Emperor regretted. For the last fifteen years Germany has been running with blood, and men have quoted the Bible as they hacked each other to pieces. And at this moment, just when Christianity is being shrivelled into little enclaves by plague, war and the Reformation, a rumour is going through Europe that you have made a secret pact with Protestant Sweden in order to weaken the Catholic emperor. So what do these wretched mathematicians do but go and point their tubes at the sky and inform the whole world that your Holiness is hopelessly at sea in the one area nobody has yet denied you? There's every reason to be surprised at this sudden interest in an obscure subject like astronomy. Who really cares how these spheres rotate? But thanks to the example of this wretched Florentine all Italy, down to the last stable boy, is now gossiping about the phases of Venus, nor can they fail at the same time to think about a lot of other irksome things that schools and others hold to be incontrovertible. Given the weakness of their flesh and their liability to excesses of all kinds, what would the effect be if they were to believe in nothing but their own reason, which this maniac has set up as the sole tribunal? They would start by wondering if the sun stood still over Gibeon, then extend their filthy scepticism to the offertory box. Ever since they began voyaging across the seas – and I've nothing against that – they have placed their faith in a brass ball they call a compass, not in God. This fellow Galileo was writing about machines even when he was young. With machines they hope to work miracles. What sort? God anyhow is no longer necessary to them, but what kind of miracle is it to be? The abolition of top and bottom, for one. They're not needed any longer. Aristotle, whom they otherwise regard as a dead duck, has said – and they quote this – that once the shuttle weaves by itself and the plectrum plays the zither of its own accord, then masters would need no apprentice and lords no servants. And they think they are already there. This evil man knows what he is up to when he writes his astronomical works not in Latin but in the idiom of fishwives and wool merchants.

THE POPE: That's very bad taste; I shall tell him.

THE INQUISITOR: He agitates some of them and bribes others. The north Italian ports are insisting more and more that they must have Mr Galilei's star charts for their ships. We'll have to give in to them, material interests are at stake.

THE POPE: But those star charts are based on his heretical theories. They presuppose certain motions on the part of the heavenly bodies which are impossible if you reject his doctrine. You can't condemn the doctrine and accept the charts.

THE INQUISITOR: Why not? It's the only way.

THE POPE: This shuffling is getting on my nerves. I cannot help listening to it.

THE INQUISITOR: It may speak to you more persuasively than I can, your Holiness. Are all these people to leave here with doubt in their hearts.

THE POPE: After all the man is the greatest physicist of our time, the light of Italy, and not just any old crank. He has friends. There is Versailles. There's the Viennese Court. They'll call Holy Church a cesspool of decomposing prejudices. Hands off him!

THE INQUISITOR: Practically speaking one wouldn't have to push it very far with him. He is a man of the flesh. He would give in immediately.

THE POPE: He enjoys himself in more ways than any man I have ever met. His thinking springs from sensuality. Give him an old wine or a new idea, and he cannot say no. But I won't have any condemnation of the physical facts, no war cries of 'Up the Church' 'Up Reason'. I let him write his book on condition that he finished it by saying that the last word lay with faith, not science. He met that condition.

THE INQUISITOR: But how? His book shows a stupid man, representing the view of Aristotle of course, arguing with a clever one who of course represents Mr Galilei's own; and which do you think, your Holiness, delivers the final remark?

THE POPE: What did you say? Well, which of them expresses our view?

THE INQUISITOR: Not the clever one.

THE POPE: Yes, that is an impertinence. All this stamping in the corridors is really unbearable. Is the whole world coming here?

THE INQUISITOR: Not the whole of it but its best part.

Pause. The Pope is now in his full robes.

THE POPE: At the very most he can be shown the instruments.

THE INQUISITOR: That will be enough your Holiness. Instruments are Mr Galilei's speciality.

13

Before the Inquisition, on June 22nd 1633, Galileo recants his doctrine of the motion of the earth

June twenty-second, sixteen thirty-three
A momentous day for you and me.
Of all the days that was the one
An age of reason could have begun.

In the Florentine ambassador's palace in Rome. Galileo's pupils are waiting for news. Federzoni and the little monk are playing new-style chess with its sweeping moves. In one corner Virginia kneels saying the Ave Maria.

THE LITTLE MONK: The Pope wouldn't receive him. No more discussions about science.

FEDERZONI: That was his last hope. It's true what he told him years back in Rome when he was still Cardinal Barberini: We need you. Now they've got him.

ANDREA: They'll kill him. The Discorsi will never get finished.

FEDERZONI *gives him a covert look*: You think so?

ANDREA: Because he'll never recant.

Pause

THE LITTLE MONK: You keep getting quite irrelevant thoughts when you can't sleep. Last night for instance I kept on thinking, he ought never to have left the Venetian Republic.

ANDREA: He couldn't write his book there.

FEDERZONI: And in Florence he couldn't publish it.

Pause

THE LITTLE MONK: I also wondered if they'd let him keep his little stone he always carries in his pocket. His proving stone.

FEDERZONI: You don't wear pockets where they'll be taking him.

ANDREA *shouting*: They daren't do that! And even if they do he'll not recant. 'Someone who doesn't know the truth is just thick-headed. But someone who does know it and calls it a lie is a crook.'

FEDERZONI: I don't believe it either and I wouldn't want to go on living if he did it. But they do have the power.

ANDREA: Power can't achieve everything.

FEDERZONI: Perhaps not.

THE LITTLE MONK *softly*: This is his twenty-fourth day in prison. Yesterday was the chief hearing. And today they're sitting on it. *Aloud, as Andrea is listening*: That time I came to see him here two days after the decree we sat over there and he showed me the little Priapus by the sundial in the garden – you can see it from here – and he compared his own work with a poem by Horace which cannot be altered either. He talked about his sense of beauty, saying that was what forced him to look for the truth. And he quoted the motto 'Hieme et aestate, et prope et procul, usque dum vivam et ultra'. And he was referring to truth.

ANDREA *to the little monk*: Have you told him the way he stood in the Collegium Romanum when they were testing

his tube? Tell him! *The little monk shakes his head.* He behaved just as usual. He had his hands on his hams, thrust
out his tummy and said 'I would like a bit of reason, please,
gentlemen.'
Laughing, he imitates Galileo.
Pause

ANDREA *referring to Virginia*: She is praying that he'll
recant.

FEDERZONI: Leave her alone. She's been all confused ever
since they spoke to her. They brought her father confessor
down from Florence.

The individual from the Grand-Ducal palace in Florence enters.

INDIVIDUAL: Mr Galilei will be here shortly. He may need a
bed.

FEDERZONI: Have they released him?

INDIVIDUAL: It is expected that Mr Galilei will recant
around five o'clock at a full sitting of the Inquisition. The
great bell of St Mark's will be rung and the text of his
recantation will be proclaimed in public.

ANDREA: I don't believe it.

INDIVIDUAL: In view of the crowds in the streets Mr Galilei
will be brought to the garden gate here at the back of the
palace.
Exit

ANDREA *suddenly in a loud voice*: The moon is an earth and has
no light of its own. Likewise Venus has no light of its own
and is like the earth and travels round the sun. And four
moons revolve round the planet Jupiter which is on a level
with the fixed stars and is unattached to any crystal sphere.
And the sun is the centre of the cosmos and motionless, and
the earth is not the centre and not motionless. And he is the
one who showed us this.

THE LITTLE MONK: And no force will help them to make
what has been seen unseen.
Silence

FEDERZONI *looks at the sundial in the garden.* Five o'clock.

Virginia prays louder.

ANDREA : I can't wait any more. They're beheading the truth. *He puts his hands over his ears, as does the little monk. But the bell is not rung. After a pause filled only by Virginia's murmured prayers, Federzoni shakes his head negatively. The others let their hands drop.*

FEDERZONI *hoarsely*: Nothing. It's three minutes past the hour.

ANDREA : He's holding out.

THE LITTLE MONK : He's not recanting.

FEDERZONI: No. Oh, how marvellous for us! *They embrace. They are ecstatically happy.*

ANDREA : So force won't do the trick. There are some things it can't do. So stupidity has been defeated, it's not invulnerable. So man is not afraid of death.

FEDERZONI : This truly is the start of the age of knowledge. This is the hour of its birth. Imagine if he had recanted.

THE LITTLE MONK : I didn't say, but I was worried silly. O ye of little faith!

ANDREA : But I knew.

FEDERZONI : Like nightfall in the morning, it would have been.

ANDREA : As if the mountain had said 'I'm a lake'.

THE LITTLE MONK *kneels down weeping*: Lord, I thank thee.

ANDREA : But today everything is altered. Man, so tormented, is lifting his head and saying 'I can live'. Such a lot is won when even a single man gets to his feet and says No. *At this moment the bell of Saint Mark's begins to toll. All stand rigid.*

VIRGINIA *gets up*: The bell of Saint Mark's. He is not damned!

From the street outside we hear the crier reading Galileo's recantation:

CRIER'S VOICE : 'I, Galileo Galilei, teacher of mathematics and physics in Florence, abjure what I have taught, namely that the sun is the centre of the cosmos and motionless and the earth is not the centre and not motionless. I foreswear, detest and curse, with sincere heart and unfeigned faith, all these errors and heresies as also any error and any further opinion repugnant to Holy Church.'

It grows dark.

When the light returns the bell is still tolling, but then stops.

Virginia has left. Galileo's pupils are still there.

FEDERZONI: You know, he never paid you for your work. You could never publish your own stuff or buy yourself new breeches. You stood for it because it was 'working for the sake of science'.

ANDREA *loudly*: Unhappy the land that has no heroes!

Galileo has entered, so completely changed by his trial as to be almost unrecognisable. He has heard Andrea's remark. For a few moments he stands at the gate waiting to be greeted. When he is not, and his pupils back away from him, he goes slowly and, on account of his bad eyes, uncertainly forward till he finds a stool and sits down.

ANDREA: I can't look at him. Get him away.

FEDERZONI: Calm down.

ANDREA *yells at Galileo*: Wine-pump! Snail-eater! Did you save your precious skin? *Sits down*: I feel ill.

GALILEO *quietly*: Give him a glass of water.

The little monk fetches Andrea a glass of water from outside. The others do nothing about Galileo, who sits on his stool and listens. Outside the crier's voice can again be heard in the distance.

ANDREA: I think I can walk with a bit of help.

They escort him to the door. At this juncture Galileo starts to speak.

GALILEO: No. Unhappy the land where heroes are needed.

A reading before the curtain:

Is it not obvious that a horse falling from a height of three or four ells will break its legs, whereas a dog would not suffer any damage, nor would a cat from a height of eight or nine ells, nor a cricket from a tower nor an ant even if it were to fall from the moon? And just as smaller animals are comparatively stronger than larger ones, so small plants too stand up better: an oak tree two hundred ells high cannot sustain its branches in the same proportion as a small oak tree, nor can nature let a horse grow as large as twenty horses or produce a giant ten times the size of man unless it changes all the proportions of the limbs and especially of the bones, which would have to be strengthened far beyond the size demanded by mere proportion. – The common assumption that large and small machines are equally durable is apparently erroneus.

Galileo. Discorsi.

14

1633–1642. Galileo Galilei lives in a house in the country near Florence, a prisoner of the Inquisition till he dies. The 'Discorsi'

A large room with table, leather chair and globe. Galileo, old now and half blind, is carefully experimenting with a bent wooden rail and a small ball of wood. In the antechamber sits a monk on guard. There is a knock at the door. The monk opens it and a peasant comes in carrying two plucked geese. Virginia emerges from the kitchen. She is now about forty years old.

THE PEASANT: They told me to deliver these.

VIRGINIA: Who? I didn't order any geese.

THE PEASANT: They told me to say it was someone passing through. *Exit. Virginia looks at the geese in amazement. The monk takes them from her and examines them dubiously. Then he gives them back to her, satisfied, and she carries them by their necks to Galileo in the large room.*

VIRGINIA: Somebody passing through has sent us a present.

GALILEO: What is it?

VIRGINIA: Can't you see?

GALILEO: No. *He walks over.* Geese. Any name on them?

VIRGINIA: No.

GALILEO *takes one of the geese from her*: Heavy. I could eat some of that.

VIRGINIA: Don't tell me you're hungry again; you've just had your supper. And what's wrong with your eyes this time? You should have been able to see them from where you are.

GALILEO: You're in the shadow.

VIRGINIA: I'm not in the shadow. *She takes the geese out.*

GALILEO: Put thyme with them, and apples.

VIRGINIA *to the monk*: We'll have to get the eye doctor in. Father couldn't see the geese from his table.

THE MONK: Not till I've cleared it with Monsignor Carpula. Has he been writing again?

VIRGINIA: No. He dictated his book to me, as you know. You've had pages 131 and 132, and those were the last.

THE MONK: He's an old fox.

VIRGINIA: He's doing nothing contrary to instructions. His repentance is genuine. I'll keep an eye on him. *She gives him the geese.* Tell them in the kitchen they're to fry the liver with an apple and an onion. *She goes back into the large room.* And now let's consider our eyes and leave that ball alone and dictate just a bit more of our weekly letter to the archbishop.

GALILEO: I'm not well enough. Read me some Horace.

VIRGINIA: Only last week Monsignor Carpula was telling me – and we owe him so much, you know; another lot of vegetables only the other day – that the archbishop keeps asking him what you think of those questions and quotations he sends you.

She has sat down to take dictation.

GALILEO: Where had I got to?

VIRGINIA: Section four: with respect to Holy Church's policy concerning the unrest in the Arsenal in Venice I agree with the attitude adopted by Cardinal Spoletti towards the disaffected rope-makers . . .

GALILEO: Yes. *He dictates*: I agree with the atittude adopted by Cardinal Spoletti towards the disaffected rope-makers, namely that it is better to hand out soup to them in the name of Christian brotherly love than to pay them more for their hawsers and bell ropes. Especially as it seems wiser to encourage their faith rather than their acquisitiveness. The apostle Paul says 'Charity never faileth'. – How's that?

VIRGINIA: That's wonderful, father.

GALILEO: You don't think a suspicion of irony might be read into it?

VIRGINIA: No, the archbishop will be delighted. He is so practical.

GALILEO: I trust your judgement. What's next?

VIRGINIA: A most beautiful saying: 'When I am weak then I am strong'.

GALILEO: No comment.

VIRGINIA: Why not?

GALILEO: What's next?

VIRGINIA: 'And to know the love of Christ, which passeth knowledge'. Saint Paul's Epistle to the Ephesians, iii, 19.

GALILEO: I am particularly grateful to your Eminence for the splendid quotation from the Epistle to the Ephesians. Stimulated by it I looked in our incomparable *Imitation* and found the following. *He quotes by heart*: 'He to whom speaketh the eternal word is free from much questioning.' May I take this opportunity to refer to my own affairs? I am still blamed for once having written an astronomical work in the language of the market-place. It was not my intention thereby to propose or approve the writing of books on infinitely more important matters, such as theology, in the jargon of pasta merchants. The argument for holding services in Latin – that it is a universal language and allows every nationality to hear holy mass in exactly the same way – seems to me a shade unfortunate in that our ever-present cynics might say this prevents any nationality from understanding the text. The cheap vulgarisation of sacred matters is something I can gladly do without. The church's Latin, which protects its eternal verities from the curiousity of the ignorant, inspires confidence when spoken by the priestly sons of the lower classes in the accents of the appropriate local dialect. – No, strike that out.

VIRGINIA: All of it?

GALILEO: Everything after the pasta merchants.
There is a knock at the door. Virginia goes into the antechamber. The monk opens. It is Andrea Sarti. He is now a man in his middle years.

ANDREA: Good evening. I am leaving Italy to do research in Holland and they asked me to look him up on the way through so I can say how he is.

VIRGINIA: I don't know that he'll want to see you. You never came.

ANDREA: Ask him. *Galileo has recognised his voice. He sits motionless. Virginia goes in to him.*

GALILEO: Is that Andrea?

VIRGINIA: Yes. Shall I send him away?

GALILEO *after a moment*: Show him in.
Virginia brings Andrea in.

VIRGINIA *to the monk*: He's harmless. Used to be his pupil. So now he's his enemy.

GALILEO: Leave us, Virginia.

VIRGINIA: I want to hear what he's got to say. *She sits down.*

ANDREA *coolly*: How are you?

GALILEO: Come closer. What are you doing now? Tell us about your work. I'm told you're on hydraulics.

ANDREA: Fabricius in Amsterdam has commissioned me to inquire about your health.

Pause

GALILEO: My health is good. They pay me every attention.

ANDREA: I am glad I can report that your health is good.

GALILEO: Fabricius will be glad to hear it. And you can tell him that I live in corresponding comfort. The depth of my repentance has earned me enough credit with my superiors to be permitted to conduct scientific studies on a modest scale under clerical supervision.

ANDREA: That's right. We too heard that the church is more than pleased with you. Your utter capitulation has been effective. We understand the authorities are happy to note that not a single paper expounding new theories has been published in Italy since you toed the line.

GALILEO *listening*: Unhappily there are still countries not under the wing of the church. I'm afraid the condemned doctrines are being pursued there.

ANDREA: There too your recantation caused a setback most gratifying to the church.

GALILEO: Really? *Pause*. Nothing from Descartes? No news from Paris?

ANDREA: On the contrary. When he heard about your recantation he shoved his treatise on the nature of light away in a drawer.

Long pause.

GALILEO: I feel concern for certain scientific friends whom I led into error. Did they learn anything from my recantation?

ANDREA: The only way I can do research is by going to Holland. They won't permit the ox anything that Jove won't permit himself.

GALILEO: I see.

ANDREA: Federzoni is back to grinding lenses in some shop in Milan.

GALILEO *laughs*: He doesn't know Latin.

ANDREA: Fulganzio, our little monk, has given up science and gone back to the bosom of the church.

GALILEO: Yes. *Pause.*

GALILEO: My superiors hope to achieve a spiritual cure in my case too. I am progressing better than anyone expected.

ANDREA: Indeed.

VIRGINIA: The Lord be praised.

GALILEO *roughly*: See to the geese, Virginia.

Virginia goes out angrily. The monk speaks to her as she passes.

THE MONK: I don't like that man.

VIRGINIA: He's harmless. You heard them. *Walking away*: There's some fresh goats-milk cheese arrived.

The monk follows her out.

ANDREA: I have to travel all night if I'm to cross the frontier early tomorrow. May I go?

GALILEO: I don't know why you came, Sarti. Was it to unsettle me? I've been living prudently and thinking prudently since coming here. Even so I get relapses.

ANDREA: I have no wish to arouse you, Mr Galilei.

GALILEO: Barberini called it the itch. He wasn't entirely free of it himself. I've been writing again.

ANDREA: Indeed.

GALILEO: I finished the 'Discorsi'.

ANDREA: What? The 'Discourses Concerning Two New Sciences: Mechanics and Local Motion'? Here?

GALILEO: Oh, they let me have pens and paper. My masters aren't stupid. They realise that deeply engrained vices can't be snapped off just like that. They shield me from any undesirable consequences by locking the pages away as I write them.

ANDREA: O God!

GALILEO: Did you say something?

ANDREA: They're making you plough water. They allow you pens and paper to keep you quiet. How can you possibly write when you know that's the purpose?

GALILEO: Oh, I'm a creature of habit.

ANDREA: The 'Discorsi' in the hands of the monks! With Amsterdam and London and Prague all slavering for it!

GALILEO: I can hear Fabricius grumbling away, insisting on his pound of flesh, meanwhile sitting safe and sound himself in Amsterdam.

ANDREA: Two new branches of science as good as lost!

GALILEO: It will no doubt relieve him and one or two others to hear that I've been risking the last pathetic remnants of my own comfort by making a transcript, more or less behind my back, by squeezing the very last ounce of light out of each reasonably clear night for the past six months.

ANDREA: You've got a transcript?

GALILEO: So far my vanity has stopped me destroying it.

ANDREA: Where is it?

GALILEO: 'If thine eye offend thee, pluck it out'. Whoever wrote that knew more about comfort than me. I suppose it's the height of folly to part with it. However, as I haven't managed to keep clear of scientific work you people might as well have it. The transcript is inside that globe. Should you think of taking it to Holland you would of course have to bear the entire responsibility. In that case you would have bought it from someone who had access to the original in the Holy Office.

Andrea has gone to the globe. He takes out the transcript.

ANDREA: The 'Discorsi'! *He leafs through the manuscript. Reads*: 'It is my purpose to establish an entirely new science in regard to a very old problem, namely, motion. By means of experiments I have discovered some of its properties, which are worth knowing.'

GALILEO: I had to do something with my time.

ANDREA: This will found a new physics.

GALILEO: Stuff it under your coat.

ANDREA: And we thought you had deserted! No voice against you was louder than mine!

GALILEO: Very proper. I taught you science and I denied the truth.

ANDREA: This alters everything. Everything.

GALILEO: Really?

ANDREA: You were hiding the truth. From the enemy. Even in matters of ethics you were centuries ahead of us.

GALILEO: Elaborate that, will you Andrea?

ANDREA: Like the man in the street we said 'He'll die, but he'll never recant.' You came back: 'I've recanted, but I'm going to live.' – 'Your hands are stained', we said. You're saying: 'Better stained than empty'.

GALILEO: Better stained than empty. Sounds realistic. Sounds like me. New science, new ethics.

ANDREA: I of all people should have known. I was eleven when you sold another man's telescope to the Venetian Senate. And I saw you put that instrument to immortal use. Your friends shook their heads when you bowed to that boy in Florence: science gained an audience. Even then you used to laugh at heroes. 'People who suffer are boring' you said. 'Misfortune comes from miscalculation'. And 'When there are obstacles the shortest line between two points may be a crooked one.'

GALILEO: I remember.

ANDREA: So in '33 when you chose to recant a popular point in your doctrine I ought to have known that you were simply backing out of a hopeless political wrangle in order to get on with the real business of science.

GALILEO: Which is . . .

ANDREA: Studying the properties of motion, mother of those machines which alone are going to make the earth so good to live on that heaven can be cleared away.

GALILEO: Aha.

ANDREA: You gained the leisure to write a scientific work which could be written by nobody else. If you had ended up at the stake in a halo of flames the other side would have won.

GALILEO: They did win. And there is no scientific work that can only be written by one particular man.

ANDREA: Why did you recant, then?

GALILEO: I recanted because I was afraid of physical pain.

ANDREA: No!

GALILEO: They showed me the instruments.

ANDREA: So it wasn't planned?

GALILEO: It was not.

Pause.

ANDREA *loudly*: Science makes only one demand: contribution to science.

GALILEO: And I met it. Welcome to the gutter, brother in science and cousin in betrayal! Do you eat fish? I have fish. What stinks is not my fish but me. I sell out, you are a buyer. O irresistible glimpse of the book, the sacred commodity! The mouth waters and the curses drown. The great whore of Babylon, the murderous beast, the scarlet woman, opens her thighs and everything is altered. Blessed be our horse-trading, whitewashing, death-fearing community!

ANDREA: Fearing death is human. Human weaknesses don't matter to science.

GALILEO: Don't they? – My dear Sarti, even as I now am I think I can still give you a tip or two as to what matters to that science you have dedicated yourself to.

A short pause

GALILEO *professorially, folding his hands over his stomach*:
In my spare time, of which I have plenty, I have gone over my case and considered how it is going to be judged by that world of science of which I no longer count myself a member. Even a wool merchant has not only to buy cheap and sell dear but also to ensure that the wool trade continues unimpeded. The pursuit of science seems to me to demand particular courage in this respect. It deals in knowledge procured through doubt. Creating knowledge

for all about all, it aims to turn all of us into doubters. Now the bulk of the population is kept by its princes, landlords and priests in a pearly haze of superstition and old saws which cloak what these people are up to. The poverty of the many is as old as the hills, and from pulpit and lecture platform we hear that it is as hard as the hills to get rid of. Our new art of doubting delighted the mass audience. They tore the telescope out of our hands and trained it on their tormentors, the princes, landlords and priests. These selfish and domineering men, having greedily exploited the fruits of science, found that the cold eye of science had been turned on a primaeval but contrived poverty that could clearly be swept away if they were swept away themselves. They showered us with threats and bribes, irresistible to feeble souls. But can we deny ourselves to the crowd and still remain scientists? The movements of the heavenly bodies have become more comprehensible, but the peoples are as far as ever from calculating the moves of their rulers. The battle for a measurable heaven has been won thanks to doubt; but thanks to credulity the Rome housewife's battle for milk will be lost time and time again. Science, Sarti, is involved in both these battles. A human race which shambles around in a pearly haze of superstition and old saws, too ignorant to develop its own powers, will never be able to develop those powers of nature which you people are revealing to it. To what end are you working? Presumably for the principle that science's sole aim must be to lighten the burden of human existence. If the scientists, brought to heel by self-interested rulers, limit themselves to piling up knowledge for knowledge's sake, then science can be crippled and your new machines will lead to nothing but new impositions. You may in due course discover all that there is to discover, and your progress will nonetheless be nothing but a progress away from mankind. The gap between you and it may one day become so wide that your cry of triumph at some new achievement will be echoed by a universal cry of horror. – As a scientist I had a unique opportunity. In my day astronomy emerged into the market place. Given this unique situation, if one man had put up a fight it might have had tremendous repercussions. Had I stood firm the scientists could have developed something like the doctors' Hippocratic oath, a vow to use their knowledge exclusively for mankind's benefit. As things are, the best that can be hoped for is a race of inventive dwarfs who can be hired for any purpose. What's more, Sarti, I have come to the conclusion that I was never in any real danger. For a few years I was as strong as the authorities. And I handed my knowledge to those in power for them to use, fail to use, misuse – whatever best suited their objectives.

Virginia has entered with a dish and come to a standstill.

GALILEO: I betrayed my profession. A man who does what I did cannot be tolerated in the ranks of science.

VIRGINIA: You are accepted in the ranks of the faithful.

She moves on and puts the dish on the table.

GALILEO: Correct. – Now I must eat.

Andrea holds out his hand. Galileo sees the hand but does not take it.

GALILEO: You're a teacher yourself now. Can you afford to take a hand like mine? *He goes to the table.* Somebody passing through sent me some geese. I still enjoy eating.

ANDREA: So you no longer believe a new age has started?

GALILEO: On the contrary – Look out for yourself when you pass through Germany, with the truth under your coat.

ANDREA *unable to tear himself away*: About your opinion of the author we were talking about. I don't know how to answer. But I cannot think your devastating analysis will be the last word.

GALILEO: Thank you very much, sir. *He begins eating.*

VIRGINIA *escorting Andrea out*: We don't like visitors from the past. They excite him.

Andrea leaves. Virginia comes back.

GALILEO: Got any idea who might have sent the geese?
VIRGINIA: Not Andrea.
GALILEO: Perhaps not. What's the night like?
VIRGINIA *at the window*: Clear.

15

1637. Galileo's book, the 'Discorsi' crosses the Italian frontier

> The great book o'er the border went
> And, good folk, that was the end.
> But we hope you'll keep in mind
> He and I were left behind.
> May you now guard science's light
> Kindle it and use it right
> Lest it be a flame to fall
> Downward to consume us all.
> Yes, us all.

Little Italian frontier town in the early morning. Children are playing by the barrier. Andrea, standing beside a coachman, is waiting to have his papers checked by the frontier guards. He is sitting on a small box reading Galileo's manuscript. On the other side of the barrier stands the coach.

THE CHILDREN *sing*:

> Mary, Mary sat her down
> Had a little old pink gown
> Gown was shabby and bespattered.
> But when chilly winter came
> Gown went round her just the same.
> Bespattered don't mean tattered.

THE FRONTIER GUARD: Why are you leaving Italy?

ANDREA: I'm a scholar.

THE FRONTIER GUARD *to his clerk*: Put under 'reason for leaving': scholar.

I must examine your luggage.

He does so

THE FIRST BOY *to Andrea*: Better not sit there. *He points to the hut outside which Andrea is sitting.* There's a witch lives inside.

THE SECOND BOY: Old Marina's no witch.

THE FIRST BOY: Want me to twist your wrist?

THE THIRD BOY: Course she's one. She flies through the air at night.

THE FIRST BOY: And why won't anyone in the town let her have a jug of milk even, if she's not a witch?

THE SECOND BOY: Who says she flies through the air? It can't be done. *To Andrea*: Can it?

THE FIRST BOY *referring to the second*: That's Giuseppe. He doesn't know a thing because he doesn't go to school because his trousers need patching.

THE FRONTIER GUARD: What's that book you've got?

ANDREA *without looking up*: It's by Aristotle, the great philosopher.

THE FRONTIER GUARD *suspiciously*: Who's he when he's at home?

ANDREA: He's been dead for years.

The boys mock Andrea's reading by walking round as if they were meanwhile reading books.

THE FRONTIER GUARD *to the clerk*: Have a look if there's anything about religion in it.

THE CLERK *turning the pages*: I can't see nothing.

THE FRONTIER GUARD: All this searching's a bit of a waste of time anyway. Nobody who wanted to hide something would put it under our noses like that. *To Andrea*: You're to sign that we've examined it all.

Andrea gets up reluctantly and accompanies the frontier guard into the house, still reading.

THE THIRD BOY *to the clerk, pointing at the box*: There's that too, see?

THE CLERK: Wasn't it there before?

THE THIRD BOY: The devil put it there. It's a box.

THE SECOND BOY: No, it belongs to that foreigner.

THE THIRD BOY: I wouldn't touch it. She put the evil eye on old Passi's horses. I looked through the hole in the roof made by the blizzard and heard them coughing.

THE CLERK *who was almost at the box, hesitates and turns back*: Devil's tricks, what? Well, we can't check everything. We'd never get done.

Andrea comes back with a jug of milk. He sits down on the box once more and goes on reading.

THE FRONTIER GUARD *following him with papers*: Shut the boxes. Is that everything?

THE CLERK: Yes.

THE SECOND BOY *to Andrea*: So you're a scholar. Tell us, can people fly through the air?

ANDREA: Wait a moment.

THE FRONTIER GUARD: You can go through.

The coachman has taken the luggage. Andrea picks up the box and is about to go.

THE FRONTIER GUARD: Halt! What's in that box?

ANDREA *taking up his book again*: Books.

THE FIRST BOY: It's the witch's.

THE FRONTIER GUARD: Nonsense. How could she be-witch a box?

THE THIRD BOY: She could if the devil helped.

THE FRONTIER GUARD *laughs*: That wouldn't work here. *To the clerk*: Open it.

The box is opened.

THE FRONTIER GUARD *unenthusiastically*: How many are there?

ANDREA: Thirty-four.

THE FRONTIER GUARD *to the clerk*: How long will they take to go through?

THE CLERK *who has begun superficially rummaging through the box*: Nothing but printed stuff. It'll mean you miss your breakfast, and when am I going to get over to Passi's stables to collect the road tax due on the sale of his house if I'm to go through this lot?

THE FRONTIER GUARD: Right, we need that money. *He kicks at the books*: After all, what can there be in those? *To the coachman*: Off with you!

Andrea crosses the frontier with the coachman carrying the box. Once across, he puts Galileo's manuscript in his travelling bag.

THE THIRD BOY *points at the jug which Andrea has left behind*: Look!

THE FIRST BOY: The box has gone too! Didn't I tell you it was the devil?

ANDREA *turning round*: No, it was me. You should learn to use your eyes. The milk's paid for, the jug too. The old woman can keep it. Oh, and I didn't answer your question, Giuseppe. People can't fly through the air on a stick. It'd have to have a machine on it, to say the least. But there's no machine like that so far. Maybe there never will be, as a human being's too heavy. But of course one never knows. There are a lot of things we don't know yet, Giuseppe. We're really just at the beginning.

Notes

Scene I

5   *Copernicus's new Cosmogony* — Nicolaus Copernicus published his key work *De Revolutionibus Orbium Coelestium* which propounded the revolutionary theory that the sun is the centre of the planetary system in 1543.

5   *armillary sphere* — a model of the heavens according to the Ptolemaic system with the earth at the centre of a number of concentric brass rings which represent the crystal spheres on which the planets are supposedly suspended.

6   *expecting something* — Galileo implies that the change will not only be scientific, but will have repercussions on the structure of society. Reflecting on the play in 1939 Brecht asked himself:

> Am I already lying down for the night and thinking, when I think of the morning, of the one that has passed, in order to avoid thinking of the one to come? Is that why I occupy myself with the epoch of the flowering of the arts and sciences three hundred years ago? I hope not.

He writes in the night of Nazi barbarism which descended in 1933 and the morning to come was then the overthrow of Hitler, which would open the way to social revolution. In the first version of the play Galileo was a model of scientific resistance to an authoritarian regime.

7   *began with the ships* — this introduces a thematic link between scientific discovery and the development of commerce and exploration which marks the transition from feudal to bourgeois society. The references to ships and building workers were added for the Laughton version.

7   *look for ourselves* — in the late Renaissance the dogma on which the Church's authority was based was challenged by empiricism which derived its laws and principles from a sceptical examination of evidence. This initial challenge to a world view based on faith led in the eighteenth century to the rationalism of the Enlightenment, which in turn helped to bring about the French

Revolution and the Industrial Revolution. It is important to realise that Brecht saw Galileo as the key figure at the beginning of this development which led to the modern, secular, scientific world.

7 *legs like our own* — the wind of change, Brecht suggests, reveals the equality of mankind.

8 *or none at all* — Galileo has worked round to the conclusion that whereas in the Ptolemaic universe there was one centre, the earth, and on it mankind whose centre was the Pope, in the new scheme of things every man is his own centre.

9 *gawping isn't seeing* — people's widespread failure to actually see what is before their eyes preoccupied Brecht from the beginning of his career. The audience at the 1923 Munich production of *Drums in the Night* was confronted with banners saying 'Don't gawp so romantically'. Here Galileo performs the experiment with the chair to demonstrate that what Andrea thinks he sees, namely the sun rising, is not what he actually sees, which is the horizon revolving towards the sun. This contradiction is a central theme in the play. The critical attitude to evidence that Galileo recommends to Andrea here is the same attitude Brecht wants to encourage in the theatregoer with his epic theatre.

11 *estates in the Campagna* — Ludovico Marsili does not feature in the first version of the play, and first appears in the Laughton version as a 'presentable young man'. Only in the final version does he become a rich estate owner and thus the representative of the landowning class.

12 *fifteen scudi a month* — the steep increase in his fee, when Galileo discovers that he is a poor learner but rich, was inserted in the final version to show Galileo as unscrupulous.

12 *selling in Amsterdam* — the telescope was patented in the Netherlands in the autumn of 1608.

14 *Procurator* — the official in charge of the university's finances, nowadays the bursar.

14 *an unproductive art* — mathematics has no commercial value, the Procurator claims. This introduces the theme of science's relationship with commerce and industry which Brecht develops, though not perhaps as fully as he might have.

15 *Giordano Bruno* — Bruno (1548-1600) was arrested in Venice in 1593 and imprisoned in Rome where he was excommunicated and burned at the stake. He was a much-travelled Dominican priest who had early held heretical views. He was executed for advocating the Copernican system and was Galileo's immediate precursor in the field. He is often alluded to but never

again named in the play. He is the subject of Brecht's novella
The Heretic's Coat (1939) in *Short Stories* (Methuen, 1983).

16   *grovelling bodies that count* — the Procurator sketches the
situation of investigative scholarship in the rest of Italy where the
acceptance of Aristotle and the maintenance of authority are the
order of the day.

17   *difficulties for you* — the Procurator makes it clear to Galileo
that the support he can really rely on comes from trade interests,
namely the businessmen of the Republic of Venice, at that time an
independent state and the most powerful trading centre on the
Mediterranean.

17   *enjoy doing my stuff* — the theme of job-satisfaction is
introduced; the pursuit of knowledge, like eating, is a passion with
Galileo.

19   *GRACIA DEI* — The Latin for the grace of God. This gives
Galileo's last speech in the scene a fine irony.

Scene 2

19   *Virginia Galilei* — Historically Virginia was the eldest of
Galileo's three illegitimate children.

19   *Signoria* — the aristocratic governing body of the republic.

20   *patient research by your humble servant* — the dramatic
irony of Galileo's speech contributes to his characterisation as a
rogue, albeit a lovable one. His sharp practice with the telescope
is founded in fact. The instrument was patented in the Netherlands
in 1608, and Galileo probably heard of a specimen brought to
Venice the following year. Galileo's biographers accept his claim
to have improved it by applying optical laws.

20   *join battle or run away* — these comments on the naval
applications of the telescope are taken almost verbatim from
Galileo's presentation speech as translated in Emil Wohlwill's
biography, *Galileo and his Struggle for the Copernican Doctrine*,
but they are transferred to the Procurator. The connection
between science and warfare, which crucially affected the final
revision of the play, is made explicit here but is not developed in
later scenes.

21   *a certain theory* — it is rash of Galileo to mention the
Copernican theory in an official gathering like this, and Sagredo
warns him of the danger.

Scene 3

24 *for a few scudi* — the point is that the availability of Dutch telescopes means that the monopoly the Venetians had been rubbing their hands over does not exist.

26 *most of my ideas* — Brecht presents Galileo as a bon viveur and even suggests that his passions for knowledge and for food and drink are interdependent. His style, if he could afford it, would be wine, food and good books.

26 *the man they burned talked about* — the man was Giordano Bruno.

27 *The stage darkens* — Brecht used constant bright light for his productions at the Berliner Ensemble. When he lowered the lights it was not for atmospheric effects, but as here, to denote the passage of time.

27 *the other fellow* — this is again Giordano Bruno, whom Galileo never names. Note the clarity with which Brecht distils complex issues into simple demonstrations and the excitement they generate.

28 *Within ourselves or nowhere* — like Giordano Bruno, Galileo has divorced belief in God from any spatial location of heaven in the revealed universe.

29 *I believe in human reason* — Galileo identifies Humanity with accessibility to reason, and this makes him a forerunner of the Enlightenment. Brecht shares his faith, and his epic theatre is based on reason, in contrast to the reliance of dramatic (or Aristotelian) theatre on emotion. Both men feel that an appeal to reason will make men see in the first case the astronomical, in the other the political truth.

29 *he drops a pebble on the ground* — when a stone is released it falls to the ground and can be demonstrated to obey the law of gravity. Galileo imagines that the whole human race shares his passion for knowledge and is hence as susceptible as he to the lure of proof. Sagredo knows that unbiased scientific curiosity is the exception, not the rule. From now on Galileo will occasionally drop his pebble to reassure himself of his own rightness.

31 *It's not a toy* — Galileo has observed that Virginia is 'not bright' (p.32). He wanted to get Andrea out of bed to show him the moons of Jupiter, but his treatment of his daughter is offhand and humiliating from the start.

31 *Moving to Florence* — Florence, capital of Tuscany, was ruled by the Medici family and was a great centre of renaissance art and learning. It was one of the richest and most powerful city states in Italy. Galileo hopes that the generosity of the Grand Duke will enable him to get on with his research and to live in greater style.

32   *the seduction of proof* — Galileo believes the scholars will be seduced by proof. The proof in question is what they can see with their own eyes, but the catch is that they can only see it through his telescope. This developes the difference between gawping and seeing a stage further.

33   *when mankind sees the truth* — Sagredo's speech is an eloquent and persuasive statement of the dangers inherent in Galileo's course. He invokes power, an element in the social equation that Galileo overlooks because it does not interest him. The sceptical axiom on which Sagredo's view is based, namely that those who have power will not tolerate a fundamental challenge to their power, is more convincing than Galileo's naive belief in reason. Nonetheless Galileo's childish persistence is in character and makes for dramatic tension.

34   *will illuminate this epoch* — this letter is quoted from historical sources. The projection of texts to counterpoint the action is an epic technique. Sagredo's common sense (unrecognised by Galileo) has opened the audience's eyes, and they can only read the letter with a sinking feeling that Galileo's passion for knowledge and his taste for the fleshpots should make him capable of such a sell-out to patronage.

Scene 4

37   *miasmas* — unwholesome vapours rising from the ground which Renaissance medicine thought to be the cause of illnesses. This conversation establishes the complacency of the health authorites for scene 5.

38   *epicyclical* — following the path of a point on a circle whose centre is on the circumference of another revolving circle, that is more or less spiralling.

38   *the pleasure of a disputation* — what follows is a demonstration of pre-Galilean scientific method. Having shown Galileo's empirical science at work, Brecht now demonstrates the Aristotelian or scholastic method which the Renaissance cherished as having been handed down from the Ancients. Whereas empirical science is deductive, Aristotelian science was inductive; it made the facts match accepted principles. Hence the Philosopher's first question. Can such stars, according to Aristotle, exist?

38   *the vernacular* — the international language of learning in the

Middle Ages was Latin and scholarship in the Renaissance had
continued this tradition. Galileo has already (p.32) expressed his
faith in the common man's common sense and Brecht adds another
populist touch here and later (p.79) by keeping the scientific debate
in a language all can understand. Historically Galileo was not
interested in a mass public, but wanted to avoid putting potential
scholars off with obscure Latin.

39   *exquisite proportions* — the values inherent in the
Philosopher's opening speech are aesthetic and moral rather than
objective and physical.

39   *reasons for assuming* — this makes the a priori nature of the
Philosopher's case clear. According to his way of thinking only if
something can exist according to (his) theory will he even look to
see if it exists in fact.

41   *divine Aristotle* — the works of the Greek philosopher and
scientist (384-322 BC) such as *de caelo (On the Heavens)* had
become the supreme authority in official scholarship.

41   *The fellow had no telescope* — in the German version Galileo
speaks this line at the end of the preceding speech. In the Laughton
version it is Federzoni's, as here.

43   *evidence of their five senses* — Galileo relates working practice
in the Great Arsenal to his own methods, thus implying a
connection between the working class and empiricism which is not
lost on the Philosopher. Galileo's admiring references to the
common man stop after scene 9.

43   *look through the telescope* — Brecht makes the following
comment on the way Laughton played this part of this scene:

> After Galileo, erupting at last, has threatened to take his
> new science to the dockyards, he sees the court depart
> abruptly. Deeply alarmed and disturbed, he follows the
> departing prince in cringing servility, stumbling, all dignity
> gone. In such a case an actor's greatness can be seen in the
> degree to which he can make the character's behaviour
> incomprehensible, or at least objectionable.

Scene 5

44   *Undeterred even by the plague* — this scene, in which Galileo
refuses to leave his work for the plague, featured in the first version
of the play, was omitted by Laughton and then reinstated by Brecht
in 1956.

45 *to see you get your meals* — Mrs Sarti drops her gruff mask and reveals her devotion to Galileo by refusing to leave. In German Galileo reciprocates by shifting from the formal to the familiar mode of address here. Brecht does not develop Galileo's intriguing relationship with his housekeeper and she disappears as soon as Virginia's engagement is broken off.

48 *the clouds with the plague seeds in them* — that clouds or miasmas (cf. p.37) should cause epidemics makes the 'modern' Galileo laugh.

48 *the Ursulines* — an order of nuns who are apparently running a convent hospital in the vicinity.

49 *lucky if you get bread* — the man's response to Galileo's request for a book is sound. It is an absurd thing to ask for in the circumstances.

Scene 6

50 *extremely hilarious* — the scene could easily slide into pathos and suspense as they await the verdict, and Brecht introduces the ribaldry and play-acting of the monks to counteract this.

51 *Tycho Brahe* — Danish astonomer (1546-1601) who observed a new star in the constellation of Cassiopeia in 1572. He attempted to reconcile the Ptolamaic and Copernican systems.

52 *Principiis obsta* — quotation from Ovid's *Remedia amoris* which means resist at the outset.

53 *nothing but animals* — the monk's horror at the prospect of being reduced to the ranks of the animals is an oblique reference to Darwin's theory of evolution, a later development in empirical science. Brecht himself had no illusions about man's 'animality' and in the winter of 1937, with Ruth Berlau, he put together a volume of novellas called *Any Animal Can do It* which offered an anti-Freudian, materialistic view of sexuality.

54 *I let it rise* — Galileo's stone reiterates his faith in 'reason's gentle tyranny' (p.29)

54 *that man we burned* — this reference to Giordano Bruno works a variation on the theme of seeing and believing. The Very Old Cardinal's eyes are weak and when he looks at Galileo he sees only a heretic who should be burned.

55 *he collapses* — The Very Old Cardinal recapitulates for the last time the anthropocentric view of the universe and makes it clear that the dignity and security of the ruling class of the day is essentially linked to it. The contrast between his conceit of himself as the apple of the Creator's eye and his physical infirmity makes for grim comedy, his ranting has echoes of Nazi rhetoric. Brecht indicated that he should be played as a die-hard Tory or a Louisiana Democrat.

55 *movements of the heavens once more* — with Clavius's terse comment Galileo would appear to have won the day. Historically the Collegium Romanum of 24 April 1611 only confirmed the moons of Saturn, and not Copernicus's heliocentric universe. Far from leaving the theologians with the problem as Brecht does, Clavius left it to the astronomers to decide how the heavenly spheres have to be imagined so that the notion of their existence could continue to be accepted.

Scene 7

55 *March 5th, 1616* — a period of time separated scenes 6 and 7 but Brecht has moved them into juxtaposition to give the play a dramatic fulcrum.

56 *old-style chess* — new chess came in in the sixteenth century, but Brecht brings it in a century later as a symbol of the new age again with its open vistas and adventurous spirit.

57 *what does Galileo say* — elegant verbal duels are a feature of Brecht's mature plays. Azdak swaps proverbs with Simon in *The Caucasian Chalk Circle* and 'The song of the Great Capitulation' in *Mother Courage and her Children* is a disputation in itself. Barberini's biblical quotation corresponds to our experience of sunrise and sunset. Galileo counters with a child's misconception that the land moves and the ship stands still. Barberini then expounds the subtlety of this to Bellarmin, namely that what one sees is not necessarily true, whereas what is true may not be perceived. So paradoxically Galileo's arguments for a materialistic universe are based on interpretative vision. Seeing is not believing.

57 *run counter to the Scriptures* — Bellarmin takes a pragmatic position. Where powerful interests have a stake in the new discoveries, like the merchants in Galileo's star charts, the Church will not object, but it will defend the Bible as the basis of its own authority.

57 *Proverbs of Solomon* — The duel of proverbs sets prudence, spirituality and inertia against curiosity, vitality and progress. Brecht commented on this scene in the light of Laughton's performance:

In the brief duel of bible quotations with Cardinal Barberini,

L.'s Galileo shows, besides the fun he has with such
intellectual sport, that the possibility of an unfavourable
outcome to his affairs is dawning on him. For the rest, the
effectiveness of the scene depends on the elegance of its
performance; L. made full use of his heavy body.

58   *Two little boys* — Barberini interprets the legend of Romulus
and Remus, who were suckled by a wolf and founded Rome, in
contemporary terms. In Renaissance Rome man is as a wolf to his
fellow man, and the city provides pleasure, but not free milk.
Barberini is attempting to bribe Galileo, but the pleasures on offer
are not to his taste.

58   *motions as the simplest* — Brecht comments on this exchange:

The brief argument about the capacity of the human brain
(which the playwright was delighted to have heard formulated
by Albert Einstein) furnished L. the opportunity to show
two traits: 1) a certain arrogance of the professional when his
field is invaded by laymen, and 2) an awareness of the
difficulty of such a problem.

59   *whereas you yourself are* — Bellarmin makes a suave, elegant
and menacing statement of official policy, brooking no interruption
from Galileo as he ruthlessly exposes the connection between
church and society. This powerful characterisation of the ruling
classes contrasts with the crudeness of the Florentine scholars in
scene 4 and even more with the caricatures Brecht gives of them in
The Caucasian Chalk Circle.

60   *the Bible too* — Galileo instantly puts his finger on the flaw in
their argument: they take the Bible (i.e. God) to mean what they
think it means.

61   *Poor old Galileo hasn't got one* — Galileo has no disguise, in
other words no skill in the wiles of dissimulation at this level.
Brecht comments on Laughton's interpretation of the role here:

When the decree is read out forbidding the guest to teach a
theory acknowledged to have been proven, L.'s Galileo reacts
by twice turning abruptly from the reading secretaries to the
liberal Barberini. Thunderstruck, he lets the two cardinals
drag him to the ball as if he were a steer stunned by the axe.
L. was able to give the impression that what mainly disarmed
Galileo was the lack of logic.

Scene 8

65   *peasants in the Campagna* — the Little Monk's speech
eloquently evokes the hard lives of his parents in the plain around
Rome. It also looks at the relationship of church and society from
a new angle and suggests that the status quo is essential to the
peace of mind of the lowest social class (the cardinals have already
shown it to be essential to the survival of the ruling class).

66   *waging in Germany and Spain* — this probably refers to the
Thirty Years War though it only broke out in 1618 and this scene
is in 1616. Galileo interprets the plight of the peasants as a
consequence of exploitation, exacerbated by the Church's involve-
ment in foreign wars. This materialist and marxist interpretation is
anachronistic; it is Brecht speaking through the historical figure.

67   *a Cellini clock* — Benvenuto Cellini (1500-1571) was a
leading Italian goldsmith.

68   *a Venus without phases* — Galileo compares himself to the
Latin poet Horace and claims that depriving Venus of its phases is
like restricting a poet's choice of imagery. Scientific patterns and
aesthetic structures cannot be made to conform to the decrees of
authority. Is Brecht taking a sideswipe at literary censorship here?

Scene 9

69   *silent for eight years* — for Brecht and Laughton giving in to
the church at this stage did not constitute a betrayal. Only when
the progressive bourgeoisie formed an alliance with science did the
issue become political. Brecht says:

> At this point people knew very little about the new science,
> the cause of the new astronomy had not yet been taken up
> by the North Italian bourgeoisie, the battle fronts are not yet
> political. There may not be an open declaration on his part,
> but there is no recantation either. In this scene therefore it is
> still the scientist's personal impatience and dissatisfaction
> which must be portrayed.

69   *A very high church person* — Virginia has now been engaged
for eight years, and in that time the Grand Inquisitor's elaborate
ironies have simplified themselves in her memory to the mildly
comic notion that in astronomy the distances are too great.

70   *is a crook* — Brecht lets Galileo formulate a position from
which he himself will later be judged by the audience.

72   *De maculis in sole* — Galileo resolutely refuses to defy Rome
and investigate sunspots as Europe is clamouring for him to do. His
correspondence and the book dedication make his continuing
pre-eminence in physics clear.

76   *Things are beginning to move* — a witty variation on Galileo's
famous (if apocryphal) 'Eppur si muove' (and yet it moves).

78   *he believes it blindly* — this penetrating observation from
Mrs Sarti helps to explain much of Galileo's behaviour for example
his refusal to listen to Sagredo (p.33) or Vanni (p.88).

78   *When I get you on your own* — in this speech Mrs Sarti
lapses into the familiar mode of address in German again, hinting
at an intimate relationship which never comes into the open.

79   *olives without a thought* — this is the best hedonistic line in
the play, and probably one Brecht concurred with.

81   *Abandon hope* — Brecht parodies the inscription over the
gates of Hell in Dante's *Inferno*, 'Abandon hope, all ye who enter
here'.

Scene 10

82   *common people* — this scene was not in the first version, but
formed scene 9 of the Laughton version. Brecht commented:

> L. took the greatest interest in the tenth (carnival) scene,
> where the Italian people are shown relating Galileo's
> revolutionary doctrine to their own revolutionary demands.
> . . . It was so important to him to demonstrate that property
> relationships were being threatened by the doctrine of the
> earth's rotation that he declined a New York production
> where this scene was to be omitted.

Scene 11

87   *the north Italian cities behind you, sir* — the role of Vanni
(Matti in the Laughton version) is expanded in the final version.
His assurance of the support of the commercial cities and his offer
of his coach to take Galileo to Venice are added. Vanni, as the
representative of the progressive middle classes, embodies the
forces of social change. Brecht came to see Galileo's rejection of
Vanni's offer as his real recantation, and the point where his
character first crumbles.

88   *I can distinguish power from impotence* — this line is more than just pragmatic; Brecht is trying to achieve negative characterisation by lining up Galileo momentarily on the side of the ruling classes.

Scene 12

90   *he is robed* — this stage direction holds the visual key to the scene. As he is elaborately dressed in the vestments and appurtenances of his office as God's representative on earth, Barberini abandons science and adopts church policy as his own. The robing is a magnificent visual metaphor for the intellectual reconstruction of the man, a phenomenon that had fascinated Brecht at least since *Man Equals Man*.

91   *And abroad* — since 1618 the Thirty Years War had divided Europe into two warring camps, with the Protestant princes led by Gustavus Adolphus of Sweden and the Catholics by the Holy Roman Emperor, Ferdinand II of Austria. This conflict which devastated Germany is the setting for *Mother Courage and her Children*.

92   *lords no servants* — the Inquisitor interprets Galileo as a figurehead for the forces of social change, a role which Galileo refuses to espouse. It is ironic that Aristotle can also be pressed into the service of progress.

92   *material interests* — Brecht, as a materialist, is quick to spot materialism in the Church's approach. It will turn a blind eye to heretical principles which are of material interest to powerful sectors of society. The Inquisitor will condemn Galileo's teachings while letting their practical implications stand.

Scene 13

94   *could have begun* — Brecht's introductory verse implies that Galileo's recantation in this scene postponed the age of reason, but historically this is only true of Italy: science marched on in France and Holland. Galileo is a milestone in the history of science, not its cornerstone as Brecht implies.

95   *is a crook* — Andrea is quoting Galileo (p.75). Galileo's collaborators idolise him, but unlike his enemies, they have no idea of his weaknesses.

95   *usque dum vivam et ultra* — in winter and in summer, near and far, as long as I live and beyond.

96   *The individual* — this Inquisition secret policeman who first appears on p.86 had a contemporary flavour in 1938 (which he has retained).

97   *All stand rigid* — Brecht uses dramatic tension skilfully in this scene in which Galileo's act of abjuration takes place offstage. Suspense is followed by relief, then by jubilation and finally by disbelief which on Andrea's part turns into aggression.

98   *Unhappy the land that has no heroes* — there is great pathos in this scene in which Andrea's sense of betrayal is balanced in the audience's eyes by the change Galileo's ordeal has wrought in his appearance. Brecht made the following comment on Laughton's treatment of this episode:

> The pupils have abandoned the fallen man: 'Unhappy is the land that breeds no hero.' Galileo has to think of an answer, then calls after them, too late for them to hear: 'Unhappy is the land that needs a hero.' L. says it soberly, as a statement by the physicist who wants to take away nature's privilege to ordain tragedies and mankind's need to produce heroes.

98   *A reading before the curtain* — the pathos of the scene is broken by the reading of Galileo's scientific prose which uses common sense to dismiss a common misconception and hints at a rational way ahead.

Scene 14

99   *the 'Discorsi'* — the German has an introductory verse for this scene:

> Sixteen hundred and thirty-three till
> Sixteen hundred and forty two
> Galileo is a prisoner of the Church
> right up to his death

101   *the disaffected rope-makers* — Brecht sees only cynicism in Galileo's comments on the unrest at the Arsenal, but it is difficult not to feel that irony predominates, especially as he is commenting on what the Cardinal has done, not advising him what to do. He notes:

> . . . .L. insisted . . . . on a scene in which Galileo collaborates with the authorities in full view of the audience. . . . So he now dictates to his daughter . . . . an abject letter to the

archbishop in which he advises him how the Bible may be
used for the suppression of starving artisans.

101 *No comment* — This saying is evidently too close to home for
Galileo to comment.

102 *Fabricius in Amsterdam* — David Fabricius (1564-1617), a
Dutch clergyman who discovered the first variable star in 1596.
Historically he died before scene 9.

103 *your utter capitulation* — Andrea makes no attempt to
conceal his contempt as the word 'utter' indicates.

103 *Descartes* — René Descartes (1596-1650), French philosopher
with an interest in physics whose most famous work is the *Discourse
on Method.*

103 *Jove won't permit himself* — in this classical metaphor Galileo
is Jove and Andrea the ox.

103 *He doesn't know Latin* — the stage direction *'laughs'* was
inserted as a result of Laughton's interpretation of Galileo at this
point. Brecht comments:

> . . . . Galileo answers: 'He can't read the books': Then L.
> makes him laugh, the laugh however does not contain
> bitterness about a society that treats science as something
> secret reserved for the well-to-do, but a disgraceful mocking
> of Federzoni's inadequacies together with a brazen complicity
> in his degradation which is explained as a simple consequence
> of his inadequacy!

This is far removed from his staunch solidarity with Federzoni on
p.79 and is designed to make Galileo seem monstrous at this point.

105 *If thine eye offend thee, pluck it out* — Galileo has a fund of
biblical quotations at his finger-tips. Brecht once claimed the Bible
was the book that had most influenced his work.

106 *real business of science* — Galileo prompts Andrea into
developing the thesis that was originally at the heart of the play,
namely that the scientist has the right to manoeuver and dissimulate
in the interests of science.

107 *contribution to science* — Even when he learns Galileo's
recantation was not part of a plan Andrea still looks for a way to
exonerate him. Galileo's sarcastic comment 'O irresistible glimpse of
the book' echoes the one about 'an apple from the tree of
knowlege' (p.68) to the Little Monk, except that now cynicism
predominates.

107 *whore of Babylon* — the abusive term used in the Old
Testament for Ishtar, the Babylonian Goddess of love and fertility.

Galileo uses it here to lend force to his contempt for science for science's sake.

107   *Creating knowledge for all* — from here down to *these people are up to*, and from *These selfish and domineering men* down to *calculating the moves of their rulers* were only inserted in the 1956 version as part of the final revision which was intended to hammer home the message that science had become the dogsbody of the ruling classes instead of the servant of humanity.

109   *a race of inventive dwarfs* — this dismissive view of scientists was inserted after Hiroshima.

109   *Now I must eat* — Brecht made the following note on Laughton's acting at this point:

> Certainly nothing could have been more horrible than the moment when L. has finished his big speech and hastens to to the table saying 'I must eat now', as though in delivering his insights Galileo has done everything that can be expected of him . . . . he replies to Sarti's repeated attempts to express his regard for him with a formal 'Thank you, sir'. Then, relieved of all further responsibility, he sits down pleasurably to his food.

109   *on the contrary* — Galileo alludes ironically and anachronistically to the Third Reich which made the truth a dangerous commodity in Germany in 1938. This contemporary reference survives from the first version, though by 1956 it was meaningless in its original sense.

Scene 15

110   *Yes, us all* — the flame that could fall and consume us all is the most direct reference to the atom bomb in the play. The reference was more explicit in a prologue to the American production which Brecht entered in his diary on 1 December, 1945:

> We hope you'll lend a charitable ear
> To what we have to say, since otherwise we fear
> If you won't learn from Galileo's experience
> The Bomb might make a personal appearance.

The photographs on the following pages (by Percy Paukschta) are of the Berliner Ensemble production directed by Erich Engel and designed by Caspar Neher with Ernst Busch as Galileo.

Above: Scene 1 (p.12). Galileo hears of the Dutch telescope from Ludovico. The high, copper-clad box-set with the stark paved floor serves, with sparse furnishings, as Galileo's 'rather wretched study'.
Below: Scene 3 (p.29). Galileo at the telescope and Sagredo.

Above: Scene 4 (p.38). In Florence Galileo demonstrates the epicyclical orbit to the nine-year-old Grand Duke (seated). Beside him is the Chamberlain and slightly upstage are the Philosopher and the Mathematician. *Below:* Scene 6 (p.50). The Collegium Romanum. Galileo, stooping slightly, watches in isolation as monks feign giddiness.

Above: Scene 9 (p.73). Mrs Sarti and Virginia are sewing. Federzoni, Andrea and the Little Monk look on as Galileo conducts an experiment on floating bodies. *Below:* Scene 10 (p.85). The end of the carnival scene is dominated by a papier-mâché head of Galileo. At centre a boy displays a bible with pages crossed out.

Above: Scene 11 (p.91). Galileo and Virginia are left standing upstage as the youthful Grand Duke and his Chamberlain exit (preceded by the Cardinal Inquisitor). *Below:* Scene 14 (p.101). Galileo, now visibly an old man, dictates to Virginia while the monk keeps an eye on things.